COMPUTE!'s
COMPUTER
VIRUSES

Ralph Roberts

COMPUTE! Books
Greensboro, North Carolina
Radnor, Pennsylvania

Other Books by Ralph Roberts:

COMPUTE!'s Using Turbo Basic
COMPUTE!'s Using Borland's Sprint
The Price Guide to Autographs
Auction Action!
Analysis with Reflect
The Power of Turbo Prolog
The Word Processor Buyer's Survival Manual

Editor: Stephen Levy

Printed in the United States of America

10 9 8 7 6 5 4 3 2

Library of Congress Cataloging-in-Publication Data
Roberts, Ralph
  COMPUTE!'s computer viruses
    p. cm.
  Includes index.
ISBN 0-87455-178-1
  1. Computer viruses.   I. Title.
QA76.76.C68R62   1988
005.8--dc19   88-28556

COMPUTE! Books, Post Office Box 5406, Greensboro, NC 27403, (919) 275-9809, is a Capital Cities/ABC, Inc. company, and is not associated with any manufacturer of personal computers. IBM is a registered trademark and OS/2 is a trademark of International Business Machines Corporation. MS-DOS is a registered trademark of Microsoft Corporation. Apple and Macintosh are trademarks of Apple Computer, Inc. Amiga is a trademark of Commodore-Amiga. Atari and Atari ST are trademarks of Atari Corporation.

CONTENTS

PREFACE

What if all the data on your computer's hard disk and/or floppies *suddenly* disappears? Millions of characters of information are irretrievably gone and the only thing left in return is an infantile message like "Arf! Arf! Gotcha!"or "Welcome to the dungeon . . . beware the virus."

The destructive rampages of these terrible little hidden programs from sick minds are not limited to high risk users who download indiscriminately from pirate electronic bulletin boards. Associated Press and United Press International stories in recent months have reported that such major institutions as NASA, Lehigh University, Miami (Ohio) University, ARCO Oil, Hebrew University in Israel, and others have had computer virus attacks. Viruses can attack your system even if you don't have a telephone modem.

Like a biological virus, a computer virus can replicate itself and be spread (through the use of "Trojan horse" programs) from system to system. Trade a floppy disk with a friend and you may unwittingly be destroying large amounts of important data in your system, be it a single-user computer or a large telephone-linked network of 20,000 terminals. It's not even enough to have good backup—a timed release virus can also be in the backup disks or tape, destroying data time after frustrating time.

There have been viruses reported for all of the major brands of computers. Those with IBM and compatibles, and Macintoshes are currently the most vulnerable, but the potential threat to all machines is scary. Like vaccinating against smallpox or typhoid fever, there are prudent steps computer users can take that may very well save them hours and days of work, or even more than that.

Whether you're a single computer owner or the manager of a large area network, this book offers relief from the fear and the very real danger of a viral infection in your system. It will help you understand and implement ways to protect your system, as well as those of your friends and clients who put programs into their own systems that were copied off your disks.

Typhoid Mary was a dishwasher who, while not sick herself, spread that disease to many others. Imagine how poor Mary would be sued today. This book helps you protect yourself in many ways.

Acknowledgments

The author gratefully acknowledges all those who helped in the preparation of this book, with special thanks to: Ray Glath, Ross Greenberg, and Pam Kane.

And to those other staunch virus fighters: Ron Benvenisti, Dennis Director, Chuck Gilmore, Eric Hansen, Dr. Harold Highland, John McAfee, Mike Riemer, Howard Upchurch, Steve Tibbett, and Jeff Shulman.

And to: Stephen Levy, Claudia Earhart, Pam Williams, and all my other friends at COMPUTE! Books.

And most especially to *you*, the reader, in hopes that this book proves helpful.

1
YOUR COMPUTER MAY BE SICK!

Virus: *"Something that corrupts or poisons the mind or the soul."*
Webster's New Collegiate Dictionary

"Over one percent, or about a quarter of a million IBM PCs and compatibles are already infected," says Larry DiMartin, president of Computer Integrity Corporation, publishers of the commercial viral protection program, Vaccinate.

A computer virus is a small program, usually hidden as a code segment of a larger *host* or *Trojan horse* program. It has the ability to replicate itself, and to move from computer to computer through the transfer of disks, or by electronic communications. You're safe only if you never buy a program, never borrow a disk from a friend, never call a computer network or electronic bulletin board, never turn on and use your computer at all. In other words, the possibility of a computer viral infection cannot be eliminated totally, only minimized.

While not alive, the resemblance in the actions of a computer virus to the reproductive and infectious qualities of a biological virus is uncanny, even horrifying. Hence the name *computer virus.*

Viruses may or may not be harmful. Their effects range from the humorous to the catastrophic. A destructive virus could wipe out data it has taken you or your company years to accumulate, including backups. Whatever the effect, *someone* is messing with your system without your permission. This book helps you to: *Avoid neglect! Detect! Protect!*

One factor on our side is that a computer virus must be machine-specific. An Amiga virus isn't going to thrive in an IBM environment; a Macintosh virus can't wipe out Atari disks.

This is the good news. The bad news is that the Computer Virus Industry Association—a group of software companies who manufacture and sell antiviral products—has already identified viruses on most of the major categories of personal computers being sold today. These include over 20 different types that attack IBM PCs and compatibles, 4 are Macintosh-specific, 4 prey on Amigas, and 6 more infect other types of computer architecture.

These, of course, are just the ones that have been verified as existing. The scope of the virus problem (as evidenced by more and more reports) continues to grow. The odds are with an individual computer owner right now; however, the odds will continue to drop if things go unchecked. Next month, next year, your computer might catch a virus. It could be sick already.

Where Do Viruses Come From?

Computers have always been prone to losing large amounts of data in the blink of an eye. Equipment malfunction, operator error—the reasons are many and varied. In this crazy world, you must also add those who *deliberately* want to destroy your data. These electronic terrorists come in many stripes.

Some, like medical experimenters who may have carelessly let a biological bug escape from the laboratory, did not unleash their viruses into the world information pool intentionally.

The term *virus* was coined by a University of California graduate student, Fred Cohen. He demonstrated how to write a computer program that could infiltrate and attack a computer system in much the same way that a biological virus infects a human. Other students and educators have experimented with these nasty little codes. So have hackers (a description that used to be honorable, but now has been sullied by those few who abuse their knowledge) and various research and development groups.

An intelligence agency is not going to overlook this means of disrupting an enemy country's informational infrastructure.

It's obvious and logical that a good many governments could already be experimenting, perhaps even field testing such computer viruses.

A second group are pranksters, those individuals or groups who have a "message" to disseminate, or just pure jokers who want to mess with your system (though not necessarily destructively). The Macintosh Peace virus—supposedly benign and well-intentioned, but still frightening many computer owners—is a prime example of this.

According to a February 12, 1988 UPI report, the source of this Macintosh virus is Richard Brandow, publisher of a 40,000-circulation magazine called *MacMag*, based in Montreal, Quebec. The report quotes a spokesman for the magazine as confirming this.

The Brandow message reads:

Richard Brandow, Publisher of *MacMag*, and its entire staff would like to take this opportunity to convey their Universal Message of Peace to all Macintosh users around the world.

The message includes a small drawing of the world and is signed by a Drew Davidson.

The virus was designed to infect the Macintosh operating system and to flash the above message on the screen on March 2, 1988, the anniversary of the Mac II's introduction. To say the reaction among thousands of Macintosh users was irate is an understatement. Many hundreds of messages condemning Mr. Brandow and the Peace virus were posted in the Macintosh special interest groups on Delphi (where they still can be read in the Mac Group), Compuserve, and Genie.

In his own defense, Brandow said: "If other people do nasty things (with a virus), it is their responsibility. You can't blame Einstein for Hiroshima."

True, but the furor and uproar came from people who did not want an infectious "disease," no matter how allegedly benign, lurking in their operating systems.

Viruses maliciously designed to be destructive come from intentional electronic terrorists. These may be individuals harboring ill against a particular company or institution, or ideological organizations. If Palestinian commandos could unleash a virus that would attack Israel's computers, might they not do it? Well, perhaps they already have. A little later we'll look at the Friday the 13th virus attack first reported by the Hebrew University in Jerusalem.

Do Viruses Really Exist?

The short answer is *yes*. Prior to 1988, although viruses were reported even in the 1970's, industry pundits tended to downplay the possibility of their existence. Anything that caused fear and reduced sales of the mushrooming personal computer industry was to be assiduously avoided.

Yet, it's the very success of the industry that has provided the medium for computer viruses to grow and spread. Their existence is no longer a matter of speculation, it's proven fact, with many incidents of viral attack now documented.

The Computer Virus Industry Association lists the top five viral strains (by reported incidence) as:

Scores (Macintosh)
Pakistani Brain (IBM PC)
SCSI (Amiga)
Lehigh (IBM PC)
Merritt (IBM PC)

The National BBS Association reports 39 known viruses. Computer viruses, however, are hard to pin down and even more difficult to trace to the perpetrator. A major problem is the lack of expertise of most computer users to recognizing viral-related problems. The Computer Virus Industry Association reports the following statistics on their investigation of virus incidents:

• 94% of submissions are nonviruses.
> 30% of these are bombs, Trojans, and so forth.
> 50% are nonanalyzable (viruses tend to destroy the evidence).
> 14% are attributable to operator error.
• Half of the remaining 6% are only partial viruses.
> Missing sectors were not collected.
> The virus was partially destroyed by its activation.

• There is an unknown, but probably large, number of viruses unreported because the user assumed the problem was in the hardware or through personal error.

The problem of computer viruses is so new and still so misunderstood that many people are still reacting out of fear. In its own way, the scourge of these data-destroying viruses can have just as frightening an effect on our society as some of the most deadly biological viruses.

Imagine your bank. A place of many branches and millions upon millions of dollars in deposits, all documented by a massive computer system. What if just one of thousands of bank employees downloads a game from an electronic bulletin board somewhere and plays it on the bank's time, using one of their PC workstations which, acting as a terminal, is connected to the bank's main computer system.

The innocuous-seeming little game is a Trojan horse, hiding a malicious virus. The virus replicates and spreads through the system. A time-released monster, it doesn't show any destructive tendencies until after it has not only made many copies of itself, but is also firmly lodged on the bank's backup tapes. The virus finally activates, and destroys or modifies perhaps millions of records.

Modification is even more frightening than out and out destruction. The random changing of one digit here and one digit there is far harder to detect. But one day you, your neighbor, the guy who runs the convenience store down the street, and the lady across town with the florist shop all go to the bank. You find there is no record of your money, or your life savings has been instantly reduced from fifteen thousand to fifteen cents!

Scary? Sure it is. A major virus attack is a catastrophe just waiting to happen. Worse, it could be you or your best friend who unwittingly copied the game from a bulletin board out of state and gave it to that bank employee.

Avoid neglect! Detect! Protect!

As the onslaught of computer viruses continue, we all have a collective responsibility. It's not enough to just safeguard our own data, we must help our fellow computer owner as well.

That, again, is what this book is all about: How to institute methods of detecting and erasing any virus that may attempt to infiltrate your system and how to keep from passing along the infection.

The Jargon

Below are definitions of the terms used in this book. These terms follow the definitions issued by the Computer Virus Industry Association.

Virus: A computer virus is a small program that can lay dormant for months before performing its destructive mission, such as erasing the contents of your hard disk. The resemblance in action to biological viruses is almost uncanny. A computer virus can replicate itself and be unwittingly spread from system to system. It "infects" and hides inside of another program, such as the computer's operating system or an application program.

Activation: The final phase of the virus life cycle, during which it does whatever was programmed in as the end goal. This can be full or partial destruction of its environment, sending a message to the screen, or some other system disturbance.

Activation Period: The time of delay programmed into the virus that it waits between the initial infection and its activation.

Bomb: A program that, through intent or programmer error, malfunctions and causes destructive results.

Boot Infector: A virus that attaches itself to the boot sector of a disk, either floppy or hard.

Generic Infector: A virus that can attach itself to any general program (such as those with the extension .COM or .EXE in the IBM world).

Hacked Programs: Hacked (and also Pirated) programs are regular commercial programs whose copy protection or other normal operation has been modified. Often not intentional, the destructiveness of these programs is simply the result of a novice programmer's poor technique.

Host Program: Host programs are those to which a computer virus attaches itself. This is an executable program such as those with .COM or .EXE extensions.

Infection Detection Product: Any hardware or software product that detects virus infection after it occurs.

Infection Identification Product: Any hardware or software product that identifies specific virus strains in an infected system.

Infection Prevention Product: Any hardware or software product that prevents a virus from initially infecting a system.

Isolation: The method the virus uses to distinguish itself from the host program.

System Infector: A virus that replicates by attaching itself to operating or environment system files.

Trojan Horse: A Trojan or Trojan Horse is either a vehicle to transmit a virus into computer systems, or a destructive program on its own. Like the ancient Greeks who were supposed to have captured the city of Troy by leaving a huge wooden horse full of soldiers outside the gates, pulling such a program into your system can have similar disastrous results. A disaster may not occur for months. On the other hand, your hard disk's light may come on when the program is run (and all files erased) and an infantile message like "Arf! Arf! Gotcha!" may appear on the screen.

Replication: The process of reproduction, where the virus copies itself (or detaches) from the present host to a new one.

Worms: Worms are an earlier name for computer viruses.

2
HISTORY AND INFAMOUS VIRUSES

You cannot judge the horse by the harness.

Old Proverb

The popular press has suddenly discovered computer viruses. As is human nature with something newly learned, many reporters treat the specter of viruses and Trojan horses as a brand new horror just now looming over the horizon of the Information Age like black storm clouds billowing and brewing.

However, the lightning-cracklings presaging the storm have been around much longer than the computer industry has previously been willing to admit. In 1974, the first self-replicating code was demonstrated at the Xerox Corporation, but the problem is even older than that.

Viral History

During the sixties, when hacker was a term of respect, young people at such places as the Massachusetts Institute of Technology were doing things with computers that had never been done before. They did wondrous and glorious things like inventing the game Space War and sitting up all night coding the most elegant "hack" (program) possible, subsisting on candy bars and soft drinks. Out of this group came many of the people who first conceived of personal computing. It was these early hackers who made personal computing possible, despite all the nay saying of the big machine people. We owe them a great debt.

One honorable pursuit, in this infancy of personal interaction with computers, was to play with friends' minds by messing up their program code. Hackers won points and respect by introducing a problem that would be undetectable for as long as possible. Watching the friend go crazy as the program bombed time after time for inexplicable reasons was considered great sport.

These clandestine modifications to code were not viruses, they were *bombs* (taking immediate effect). Yet, these bombs proved that controlling another person's program to someone's own ends was possible. Perhaps the one universal rule of all mankind is if something is possible, someone, somewhere, for some reason (sane or not), will do it. We can then attach the addendum that someone else will hear of this thing being done, and do it. When a computer virus is reported in the press, other programmers may decide to construct viruses of their own.

Computer Crime

The subject of viruses is not the only one the computer industry has been silent on—another area is computer crime. A major reason for the silence is simply self-interest. The companies are afraid—justified to some extent—that talk of viruses will hurt sales, and that public discussion of computer crime will encourage other programmers to emulate it.

Some of the same techniques used in the late fifties to defraud by computer are also being used in the sick world of those who hatch and unleash computer viruses. A *logic bomb* is one of these. This is a clandestine portion of a program which is executed when the computer determines that certain conditions have been met. These conditions can be satisfied by elapsed time, the number of times the program has run, or more commonly, on a certain date.

There have been numerous instances where a programmer who quit or was fired from a large company left such a bomb in the system. These logic bombs have done such things as simply shut down the system on the programmer's birthday, in effect, taking the day off, to maliciously destroying thousands of important records. Again, if it can be done (and it certainly *can*), someone will attempt it.

It's much harder to implant an undetectable program that will accomplish a useful feat for the warped programmer—such as rounding down all cents figures and routing the overage into an account belonging to the computer burglar. It's easier to slip in a virus or bomb that will do malicious damage. Such programs usually destroy themselves and make it almost impossible to find the perpetrator.

Thus, computer viruses are a more common problem than computer crime for profit. They are also more widespread. While it may pay to slip a "round down" program into a bank's system (a task security people continue to make harder and harder), the same is not true of a personal computer system. Most likely, no one wants to steal your data, someone wants to destroy it.

The Recent Viral Explosion

The computer industry's tight lid on virus information began leaking in 1984, when scientific papers on computer viruses started appearing. The first virus to cause widespread infection and damage appeared in 1986. By 1988, public reports from Associated Press and others, and articles in the various industry trade periodicals, have caused the industry pundits not only to pull their heads from the sand, but in many cases, to glare around in a state close to panic.

Many software publishers are spurring their programmers to build in virus protection for commercial programs (and let's hope that none of those programmers become disaffected). A number of companies have sprung up who make products to detect and protect systems against viruses, and many shareware and public domain programs are also now available.

The basis for this sudden concern about viruses by the industry and the increased public awareness of the problem is the same—it's gotten worse. Literally several million more computers exist today than did a mere two years ago. Telephone modems are selling for under one hundred dollars. Tens of thousands of users are calling electronic bulletin boards and computer networks daily. The medium for computer viruses to thrive and spread has become a hundredfold more fertile. As computers continue to spew from scores of assembly lines in the many thousands per year, "living" space for viruses increases dramatically.

Let's be frank. The virus problem is going to get worse before it gets better. We're all going to have to take measures to protect ourselves and those who we come in contact with electronically. This is why the bulk of this book is concerned with actual detection and protection instead of theory.

The *Scores* Virus

The Environmental Protection Agency, NASA, and Apple Computer's Washington, D.C. sales office were all hit this year, according to the April 11, 1988 issue of *InfoWorld*. In each case, systems were affected by a virus program on personal computers within their systems (in this case, Macintoshes). It spread from there throughout the system. As reported by Bill Pike in the *Virus Newsletter*, private contractors in the Washington and North Carolina area inadvertently sold dozens of computers that carried the virus on hard disk to government agencies.

It is not yet known how much damage was done over a five month period starting in January. Damage to government data appears to be limited, due mostly to the virus being designed for personal computers while most of the sensitive data was in main frame computers that the virus couldn't infect.

The FBI was called in to investigate. Because the original source is so difficult to determine, the efforts of the investigators are being spent more on trying to prevent future occurrences rather than pinning the blame on an individual or group.

"This was definitely a criminal act," Cynthia Macon, a spokeswoman for Apple said.

The Scores virus has built in time bombs that activate at two, four, and seven days after a disk has become infected. The results are varied, but include printing problems, system crashes, and the malfunction of desk accessory operations.

Data files are not affected by this particular virus, but all application programs including system files have to be deleted to erase the virus. A government technician, who preferred not to be named, said the Scores virus had now been widely dispersed throughout the country.

Apple now admits the problem and has released an antiviral program (called Virus RX) which will be discussed later. Scores is the most commonly reported type of virus, but the IBM and compatibles world make up for this by having many more strains of viruses.

The *Brain* Virus

The Providence, R.I. *Journal-Bulletin* newspaper, in a widely-published UPI report, said it spent a week and a half stamping out a virus that infected their in-house PC network used by reporters and editors. The virus apparently destroyed one reporter's data and infected scores of floppy disks before it could be removed.

Journal reporter Jeffrey L. Hiday said the virus was "a well-known, highly sophisticated variation called the brain virus, which was created by two brothers who run a computer store in Lahore, Pakistan." Variations of this alleged virus have cropped up at companies and colleges across the country, including Bowie State College in Maryland, where it destroyed five students' disks, and Miami University in Ohio, where it threatened to wipe out stored term papers.

Hiday wrote that the newspaper contacted one of the Pakistan brothers by phone, who said he created the virus merely to keep track of software he wrote and sold, adding that he did not know how it got to the United States.

"U.S. computer programming experts, however, believe the Pakistanis developed the virus with malicious intent," Hiday wrote. "The original version may be relatively harmless, they point out, but its elegance lends itself to alterations by other programmers that would make it more destructive."

The newspaper discovered the virus on May 6 when a message popped up on computer screens reading, "Welcome to the Dungeon . . . Beware of this VIRUS. Contact us for vaccination." The message included a 1986 copyright date, two names (Basit and Amjad), a company (Brain Computer Services), an address (730 Nizam Block Allama Iqbal in Lahore, Pakistan) and three phone numbers.

The *Lehigh* Virus

Here's how Kenneth R. van Wyk, User Services Senior Consultant, Lehigh University Computing Center, described the Lehigh virus that attacked their system in 1987, destroying a large percentage of their public site disks.

"The virus is contained in the stack space of COMMAND. COM. When a PC is booted from an infected disk, all a user need do to spread the virus is to access another disk via TYPE, COPY, DIR, etc. If the other disk contains COMMAND.COM, the virus code is copied to the other disk. Then, a counter is incremented on the parent. When this counter reaches a value of 4, any and every disk in the PC is erased thoroughly. The boot tracks are nulled, as are the FAT tables, etc.

"All Norton's horses couldn't put it back together again.

"This affects both floppy and hard disks. Meanwhile, the four children that were created, go on to tell four friends, and then they tell four friends, and so on, and so on."

The *Friday the 13th* Virus

Y. Radai of the Computation Center at the Hebrew University of Jerusalem recently described the Friday the 13th virus, which also affects IBM PCs and compatibles. He did so in a warning message disseminated widely on the ARPLANET computer network (which connects government agencies, universities, and similar institutions worldwide), and which was then copied to the various commercial networks such as CompuServe and Delphi.

"Our version," Radai said (comparing it to the Lehigh virus), "instead of inhabiting only COMMAND.COM, can infect any executable file. It works in two stages: When you execute an infected .EXE or .COM file the first time after booting, the virus captures interrupt 21 (hexadecimal) and inserts its own code. After this has been done, whenever any .EXE file is executed, the virus code is written to the end of that file, increasing its size by 1808 bytes. .COM files are also affected, but the 1808 bytes are written to the beginning of the file, another 5 bytes (the string MsDos) are written to the end, and this extension occurs only once."

The disease, according to Radai, manifests itself in at least three ways:

1. Because of this continual increase in the size of .EXE files, such programs eventually become too large to be loaded into memory or there is insufficient room on the disk for further extension.
2. After a certain interval of time (apparently 30 minutes after infection of memory), delays are inserted so execution of programs slows down considerably. (The speed seems to be reduced by a factor of 5 on ordinary PCs, but by a smaller factor on faster models.)
3. After memory has been infected on a Friday the 13th, any .COM or .EXE file executed on that date gets deleted.

"It is possible," Radai continues in the message, that the whole thing might not have been discovered in time were it not for the fact that when the virus code is present, an .EXE file is increased in size *every* time it is executed. This enlargement of .EXE files on each execution is apparently a bug; probably the intention was that it should grow only once, as with .COM files, and it is fortunate that the continual growth of the .EXE files enabled us to discover the virus much sooner than otherwise.

"From the above it follows that you can fairly easily detect whether your files have become infected. Simply choose one of your .EXE files (preferably your most frequently executed one), note its length, and execute it twice. If it does not grow, it is not infected by this virus. If it does, the present file is infected, and so, probably, are some of your other files. (Another way of detecting this virus is to look for the string 'sUMsDos' in bytes 4–10 of .COM files or about 1800 bytes before the end of .EXE files; however, this method is less reliable since the string can be altered without attenuating the virus.)

"Of course, this is only the beginning. We can expect to see many new viruses both here and abroad. In fact, two others have already been discovered here. In both cases the target date is April 1. One affects only .COM files, while the other affects only .EXE files. What they do on that date is to display a 'Ha ha' message and lock up, forcing you to cold boot. Moreover (at least in the .EXE version), there is also a lockup one hour after infection of memory on any day on which you use the default date of 1-1-80. (These viruses may actually be older than the above-described virus, but simply weren't noticed earlier since they extend files only once.)"

The *Sunnyvale Slug*

An article in the July, 1988 *Personal Computing* reported that a northern California company (who prefers not to be named) was suffering attacks in their IBM PCs from a virus dubbed the Sunnyvale Slug.

The Slug does various things, some benign and some destructive. It may flash a message on the screen reading: "Greetings from Sunnyvale. Can you find me?" Worse, it sometimes modifies DOS's COPY command so it deletes instead of copies.

The company, as more and more are doing, turned to an outside virus expert to help clean their system—in this case, Panda Systems of Wilmington, Delaware. Panda manufactures a commercial virus protection program, the Dr. Panda utilities (which, along with many others, are discussed later in this book).

President Pam Kane and her programming staff serve as an equivalent in the computing field to famous oil well fire extinguisher Red Adair in the petroleum industry. If a company is suffering a viral attack in its system, Pam and her troops can "cap the fire."

Conclusion

Computer viruses exist and have existed for some time. There are many documented examples, like those above, of their attacks. The explosive spread of personal computers in their many millions give viruses a fertile medium in which to replicate and spread as well.

3
HOW VIRUSES WORK

The disaster originating in this source, spread throughout the country and the people.

Horace

Let's tell it like it is.

Computer data storage is a lot more vulnerable than most people realize. The problem of viruses, bombs, and Trojan horses aside, there are still numerous operator errors and equipment malfunctions that can scramble the contents of a floppy disk or even an entire 20 megabyte hard disk in less than a second!

Salespeople and others connected with the computer industry tend to not mention or, at best, gloss over this vulnerability. It has been the experience of this writer, wearing the hat of computer consultant, that most people are simply unaware of how precarious their data storage really is. On IBM and other MS-DOS computers, how often are disks examined with CHKDSK? Not nearly enough. Lost cluster chains and files corrupted for a variety of reasons crop up constantly on the best of systems.

An Accident Waiting to Happen

If CHKDSK is not used often to check that a disk is storing data properly—and appropriate maintenance implemented when a problem is detected—any MS-DOS file system will eventually tear itself apart. This is a fact of life.

The computer industry has greatly downplayed the areas in which computers can be unreliable. Backup and DOS-level maintenance is not stressed at all, and end users waste hours upon hours recovering data (or trying to).

Every file read/write operation is an "accident waiting to happen." Not just on IBM and compatibles, but on all computers. The disk is spinning (in the case of most PC hard disks) at perhaps 3600 rpm. The heads are whipping back and forth. There are millions of operations per second going on in the computer's memory. A momentary voltage surge, a minute mechanical slippage, an error in one of thousands of program instructions, and the data on the disk is ruined or damaged.

It is beyond the province of this book to explain DOS-level maintenance (although it's *strongly* recommended that you learn and use these techniques for your own protection), but the point to be made here is that computers are already easy enough to foul up. Because of this vulnerability, viruses can quickly and easily do serious damage—in mere milliseconds.

Disks Present a Bare Throat to Viruses

For programs to work reliably, data must be stored in a consistent manner on all computers of a specific type. The actual structure of information recorded on MS-DOS disks is different from that used for Macintosh computers (reflecting the demands of their respective operating systems), but is essentially the same for all computers within that class. In other words, an IBM PC compatible disk from a computer in Hong Kong can be read by one in New Jersey or Scotland or Pago Pago, American Samoa.

This interchangeability is both a strength and a weakness. It allows the free exchange of information, but it also facilitates the spread of viruses.

Without getting too technical, understanding how disks work (and their vulnerable nature) will show you just why viruses can have such a field day trashing your system. All disks work in the same general way, but let's use the MS-DOS (IBM and compatibles) as an example.

All disks (5¼" floppies, 3½" disks, or fixed hard disks) are all basically the same in operation. The only difference, essentially, is a matter of capacity. Each of these disks has a number of magnetic *tracks* (sometimes referred to as *cylinders*). Tracks may be thought of as similar to the grooves on a phonograph record.

Each track is subdivided into *sectors* (all of this done magnetically by the computer that formatted the disk). Tracks and sectors have specific numbers: Every part of the disk has an address.

A program can then send a request to the computer to read or write data into or out of Track X, Sector Y. This command is sent by the computer to the disk controller card, which figures out how to physically position the read/write head in order to comply with the instructions received.

Thus, if a program can send erroneous address information during a write process, data belonging to a file other than the one being worked on can be overwritten. So *any* of perhaps hundreds of programs on a hard disk can, through simple error, foul up any of literally millions of pieces of data. The disk controller has no way of knowing whether the command was right or not—or whether it came from a legitimate program or a virus—it just blindly writes to the location specified.

The first track on a disk, especially on a hard disk, usually has a small program that's read and run when you first turn on your computer. This process is called *booting* and the first track is the *boot track*. The boot program initializes the computer and readies it to do work. If the boot program is infected by a virus, you've lost control from the start.

Now for a really soft place in disk structure, the jugular vein that sharp-fanged viruses often go for—the *File Allocation Table*. After a while, disks become *fragmented*. That is, if there is a 40K file to be written but there's not 40K of contiguous space, the disk controller will break up the file and put the fragments here and there as it tries to effectively use all the space on the disk. (This, by the way, has the effect of slowing down disk accesses as the heads eventually have to hunt all over the disk to find the sectors belonging to a particular file. A utility to optimize disks, like Norton's Speed Disk, speeds up access time by simply redoing the disk so files are contained in adjacent clusters instead of randomly distributed.)

The real problem occurs because of the just-described way

in which sectors are put on disks—in any open space. For the computer, through the disk controller, to find all of our 40K file again, there has to be an index (actually, in this case, indexes).

On a MS-DOS disk, the directory structure on the first part of the disk references the first *cluster* of all files (beginning address) and another index, the FAT or *File Allocation Table.* The FAT has the other addresses for the scattered clusters that contain the remainder of the file. A cluster represents the smallest amount of information about a file that the operating system knows how to read or write.

The disk controller, when given the address (track and sector) of this cluster, can access the first portion of the file. Next, the FAT is referred to for the location of the next cluster, and so on until the end of the file is reached.

Every cluster on the disk is referenced in the FAT table. The information contained here can indicate that the cluster is unused, damaged (marked as a bad cluster), that it's the last cluster in a file, or show where the next cluster in that file is located. In other words, the FAT provides the *chain* that links clusters together to form files.

A standard 360K floppy has 354 clusters. A 24 megabyte hard disk has over 12,000. Each of these 12,000 plus clusters is referenced in the FAT for that disk. It's the only way files can be properly read or written to.

If you think all this sounds like a cumbersome, error-prone way to do things, you're right! There is no need to erase files or cause the disk to be reformatted for a virus or worm to make a disk unusable. Just trash the FAT. All the information will still be on the disk but *you can't get to it* (a good programmer, with a lot of headaches and cursing can recover parts of the disk).

Because of the delicacy and openness of your computer's read/write procedures, viruses can also do much more subtle and insidious things. If a virus is just occasionally changing data randomly, you may not even detect the problem before wholesale file corruption has set in.

Let's look now at the types of computer viruses. We'll follow up with ways to protect against viral infection and how to detect and get rid of any you might already have.

Types of Viruses

The Computer Virus Industry Association, whose members are companies manufacturing antiviral software and hardware, is one group attempting to define standard terms. There are, according to the association, currently three classes of viruses: Boot infectors, system infectors, and general executable program infectors.

Steve Gibson, the popular "Tech Talk" columnist in the computer trade weekly, *InfoWorld*, says there are *four* classes of viruses. He defines them as: General Purpose Infector (GPV), Special Purpose Infector (SPV), Very Clever General Purpose Infector Virus (VCGPV), and the Central System Infecting Virus (CSIV). The first three can infect any application program, while the last infects the operating system only.

Both classifications fit what is now known about viruses. Gibson's system, as might be expected, is the more technical. Since this book is aimed more toward the general user who just wants to protect his or her system, not become a virus expert, we'll use the Computer Virus Industry Association's definitions.

The National BBS Society has identified 39 different viruses, and there are certainly more strains than that. The good news is (despite how easily a virus can damage your system) there is only a very limited way in which this can be accomplished. A computer's disk storage techniques are wide open to interference, but there are generally only four ways in which a virus can do so. These are:

High-level format. A high level format is what happens when you use DOS's FORMAT command. This lays down the magnetic structure used to store files. While this type of damage is aggravating, you can restore the disk if you've taken the precaution of using a format recovery program like those by Norton or Mace ahead of time. High-level formatting on an already formatted disk does not actually erase data except for initializing the Directory and FAT areas. This is true for both floppies and hard disks.

Low-level format. Hard disks, when initially installed, require a process called low-level formatting. In essence, this lays down a foundation for a highllevel format. Low-level formatting *does* erase all data. You cannot do a low-level format with regular operating system commands (such as MS-DOS). Usually these are done by hard disk installation programs, or by viruses.

System operation. FAT, Directory, and Boot Sector scrambling are ways in which system operation can be played with. It takes just a few milliseconds for a virus to destroy the file allocation table, erase the directory, or overwrite the boot sector. Overwriting the boot sector is an effective way of killing a hard disk. The system simply refuses to boot up. You may get an error message such as Probable Non-DOS Disk. The system may also be slowed down and other unacceptable operations occur.

Data scrambling. The effects here are usually more subtle and may not be caught for months. Numbers are randomly changed. Customer accounts and other data become corrupted. If the computer is used for billing you may learn this immediately in a scorching phone call, or, in the case of under-billing, you may lose a lot of money before finding out you have viral problems.

Boot Infectors

The Computer Virus Industry Association's three classes of viruses are described in the online file "Anti-Virus Measures" from association member InterPath Corporation (manufacturers of C-4 and Tracer). Boot infectors attach themselves to sector 0 of floppy disks and, occasionally, hard disks. This area of the disk is part of the boot track.

Viruses that have infected the boot track gain control when the system is first turned on and remain in control at all times. Many have the capability to trap warm boot requests (holding down the Ctrl and Alt keys and pressing the Del key) and remain in control even if booted from a noninfected floppy, with the result that the clean floppy becomes instantly infected.

Boot infectors typically create bad disk sectors to which the original boot sector is copied, along with the remainder of the virus code. Boot infectors may be from 2 to 7 sectors in length.

Boot infectors can be benign or malignant. The Pakistani Brain virus (described in the previous chapter), for example, was claimed to be a benign boot infector virus in its original form. The company in Lahore, Pakistan supposedly wrote it merely as a way to keep track of their software.

Programmers refer to code that is extremely efficient for a particular task as *elegant*. The Brain virus program is elegant at doing its task of infection, and is also easy to modify into a very malignant form.

Whether it was originally meant to be this or not, the virus is now a nasty little monster that can infect hard disks and destroy FAT entries, delete files, and perform other destructive activities.

Boot infectors can do the following:

- Move or overwrite the original boot sector
- Replace the boot sector with themselves
- Create bad sectors containing virus remainder
- Infect through soft reboot (Ctrl-Alt-Del) or other functions.

System Infectors

Several kinds of viruses, again as described in InterPath's informational file, attach themselves to COMMAND.COM and other system files that remain memory resident. They gain control after system boot and infect hard disks or other bootable floppies that contain the appropriate system files.

Memory resident programs (also called TSR's for Terminate and Stay Resident) are prime candidates for infection by this type of virus. Any power user of computers has several of these programs, such as Borland's *Sidekick* on both IBM PCs and compatibles, and also for Apple's Macintosh.

However, even if you have no TSR programs in memory, the operating system probably already has. Such MS-DOS commands as COPY, DIR, and ERASE are loaded into memory when the computer boots. These miniprograms can be accessed and manipulated (to your detriment) by system infectors.

System infectors may activate after a given period of time or they may instantly begin subtle modifications in system processing—including increasing the time to perform system functions, subtle scrambling of data or modification of system error messages, or informational messages. The Friday the 13th virus first discovered at the Hebrew University in Israel is an example of such a virus. (This virus is also able to act as a general .COM and .EXE infector as well as being a system infector).

Like the time-release pills in such medicines as Contac, activation of computer viruses can take place after a specified period of time or times have elapsed. A specific number of times a program is run can also serve as a trigger. Activation may include scrambling the FAT, erasure of specific files, low level disk format, or modification of nonexecutable files containing numeric or other ASCII data.

General .COM and .EXE Infectors

General Infectors is the third and final class defined by the Computer Virus Industry Association. This class of virus is the most dangerous from an infection standpoint since these viruses can spread to almost any executable program in any system. Your spreadsheet, word processor, games, utilities, or any program you run can be a target. These viruses infect in three general ways, by

1. Gaining control each time the infected program is executed and copying itself to other .COM or .EXE files on the fixed or floppy disk prior to passing control to the host program. This is the most common infection technique. Since the drive light is already on, and the whole process takes almost no time, it's practically undetectable.
2. Remaining memory resident and infecting each program that's loaded for execution. This technique is used by the Friday 13th virus but is less common than the above method.
3. Attaching themselves externally to .COM or .EXE files and thus changing the file size. They may or may not modify the creation date and time. Others insert themselves internally in the executable host program's dead space and are thus invisible to anything other than a binary compare routine. Some viruses continue to infect the same program multiple

times until the program becomes too large to fit into memory. Most, however, check to see if the host has already been infected and pass over previously infected files.

Viruses Battling for Supremacy

Viruses, like life forms, may fight for territory and "eat" other viruses. Here's an example:

There is a public domain program called "Core War," which has been available for several types of computers including IBMs and compatibles for at least four years now. It's a computer game played both with and *by* computers. In Core War, two player-written computer programs operate concurrently in a circular memory array. A program loses when it hits an instruction it can't execute.

The information below comes from the documentation file included with the program. There is no attribution to the author of the distributed version, but COREWARS.C was written by Kevin A. Bjorke in May of 1984, in Small-C version 2.03, and placed in the public domain.

Most of us think of a computer loading a program into its working memory and running it. When we're word processing or using a spread sheet, that's all that's happening. Right? Wrong. There are still *lots* of things going on in memory, many of them unrelated to the program now running. What's worse, viruses could be battling to see which can do the most damage.

Core War is just a game, but it demonstrates the freedom viruses have in an unprotected system *once* they get into memory. Also, these types of programs can (and no doubt did) serve as the models for actual viruses. Core war programs are described more fully by A. K. Dewdney in the "Computer Recreations" column of Scientific American, May 1984. Here's a short synopsis of Mr. Dewdney's article (omitting the technicalities).

Neither program originally knows where in memory the other is, or even where the program itself has started—however, the memory array used by Core War is circular, and all addressing is relative, so absolute memory addresses are not important. Both battle programs are executed by the Core War operating system, MARS. In the version included with the IBM public domain version, MARS is also the program loader.

Programs are loaded either from the keyboard or from disk (when you give the program a name, it will check the directory for that name; if it finds it, it will load it from disk, assuming the program is an ASCII file). The MARS interpreter simply keeps switching its program counter from one program to another—ABABABABABABAB . . . until one program loses, some maximum number of instruction cycles have been performed (as a safeguard against endless loops), or you hit <ESC> to abort.

Here's the shortest possible battle program, called "IMP:"

MOV 0 1

IMP just copies the current location to the next location, then advances to the next location, and so forth. While the original program is short, it will eventually gobble up every memory location if unchecked, thus becoming the largest possible battle program as well. It can even spread to its opponent, since any program that jumps to a location written by IMP will become an identical clone of IMP.

ANTI.IMP sets up a marker byte at −5 relative to its first byte and then waits for IMP to come along. When the marker changes, it bombards the area that IMP is moving into with DAT 0 instructions, which IMP can't execute and thus "bites" it.

ANTIANTI.IMP writes a block of code that *looks* like IMP into progressively higher memory locations. When ANTI.IMP senses this drone IMP, it will attack it, but to no avail—it will still get overwritten and then become a clone of IMP. At this point it turns around and wreaks havoc on ANTIANTI.IMP, which has no protection against IMP itself.

Other examples are given in Dewdney's article, such as DWARF, which fires "Zero Bombs" in a fashion similar to ANTIANTI.IMP; GEMINI, which simply runs away; or RAIDAR, which is able to leapfrog over advancing attacks.

There may come a time, if the virus problem continues to grow at the rate it is now, when killer viruses will have to be developed. These "good" viruses might be unleashed in a computer system much as you would get an injection of antibiotics to fight an infection in your biological body.

So far, as we will see in the next chapter, eradicating viruses from a computer system follows more conventional lines. But, until the computer hardware manufacturers make systems that aren't so delicate and open to viruses, don't count on things staying the same. Viruses will escalate, and so will protective programs.

How Does Your Computer Get Infected?

A virus invades your system in a carrier or Trojan horse program. Basically there are only two ways a virus can enter your computer: You've either physically placed a disk into the machine that has a virus on it or you've downloaded a virus over the telephone or a LAN (Local Area Network).

Just doing a quick DIR (directory) of a disk (if it has a system file like COMMAND.COM on it) lets the virus jump into your computer. The infected disk may have been in the drive for only five seconds or so. It takes much less time than that for a nimble virus program. The more programs you buy or trade for, or have been given to you, the greater the chance of viral infection.

Booting from a floppy disk is even worse. InterPath, maker of the C-4 antiviral program, stresses that booting from a floppy is a high risk practice and the single largest cause of viral infection.

Calling another computer over the phone lines, such as electronic bulletin boards (BBSs) also puts you at risk if that computer is infected. The more computers you call, the greater the chance of viral infection.

However, all the above are useful things to do. Why should we let a few sick minds keep the vast majority of computer users from enjoying the fantastic benefits of telecommunications? The answer is there is no reason! In the next chapter we'll discuss ways of fighting viruses and practicing safe computing.

The Reproductive Urge

Computers, even personal computers, have become so sophisticated now that they support a very crude imitation of life cycle processes. Viruses can burrow into host programs like biological viruses into living cells. They have an urge to re-produce or replicate themselves. Like in real life, they seek the immortality given by offspring.

As are life forms, viruses are usually specialized, some strains inhabiting boot sectors, others system files such as COMMAND.COM or the hidden BIOS files, and some hardy ones that are able to exist in almost any .COM or .EXE executable program.

Like genetic codes in living microorganisms, computer viruses also have a greater instinctual reason for existence. They have the drive to reproduce, but reproduction accomplishes their final goal. That goal may be something as innocuous as flashing a humorous message on the screen, or as malignant even as a low level format of your hard disk.

A computer virus enters your system concealed in a Trojan horse carrier program. Most programs, especially large ones, have empty or unused areas in their code where a smaller program can easily be concealed.

When this Trojan horse program is run, a replicating virus will take control of it for a brief time during the start up phase. Since the disk light is already on because the program is loading, you'll probably notice nothing out of the ordinary. The virus quickly checks to find an uninfected host program. It copies itself into that one, then returns control to the program starting up, which then runs as if nothing has happened.

Such activity will happen each time the Trojan is invoked until all the programs the virus can reach are infected. At that time, the virus may trigger and do whatever goal its creator has programmed in (usually something quite nasty). Or, it may wait until a specific time, infecting any new programs you put into the system and, of course, going out with all programs you give or trade to friends, or upload to BBSs.

The more sophisticated viruses, even when triggered, do not engage in wholesale destruction. They change data randomly and degrade system performance, all while remaining hidden in the hopes of spreading to other systems. In such manner, the virus goes through many generations and can infect thousands of systems, thus achieving the goals (usually sick) of the person who programmed it.

The *Retro-Virus*

The latest virus discovered and verified by the National BBS Association is called the retro-virus. It was first publicly described by Steve Gibson in the May 9, 1988 *InfoWorld*.

Three popular shareware programs (which are not named) are the hosts for this viral strain. The programs are infected by the virus and reproduce by attaching passive carrier clones of itself to other executable programs. It rides these programs in hopes of finding one of the three programs it can live inside.

The name retro-virus was given because it communicates with the carrier clones of itself using a clever flag hidden within the system. When any of the viral clones activates, this flag is turned on. When one of the three infected programs is run, the flag is checked and turned off. If it was *already* off, the virus assumes the infected programs must have been removed from the system. Then it waits for several months to *reinfect* the target programs. Like a submarine rigged for *silent running,* the retro-virus waits until the destroyers have stowed the depth charges and gone back to port before returning to sink ships.

Conclusions

Computer viruses imitate real life viruses in the way they reproduce. On a hard disk they can infect hundreds of programs and spread to new systems as these programs are entered via disks or telephone modem. Running an infected program spreads the infection.

Viruses are becoming more and more sophisticated and already lurk in thousands of systems. The National BBS Society has identified 39 strains (most of which are on the IBM and compatibles, or Apple's Macintosh computers). It is obvious that the problem will only get worse before it gets better.

What can you do to rid your system of any viruses that may be present and to make sure no infection occurs? The remainder of this book is concerned with the specifics of detection and protection.

4
FIGHTING VIRUSES AND PRACTICING SAFE COMPUTING

When false things are brought low . . .

Thomas Hardy

The best cure for any virus is not to catch it in the first place. Alas, unless you do all your computing in an underground bunker on a totally isolated computer, and use only programs you've written and personally typed into the computer yourself, chances are your system will sooner or later be exposed to a virus, Trojan, worm, or hacked program of some sort. The Third Marine Division is useless against this kind of invasion.

This chapter gives you the general precepts needed to detect and prevent viral infections, as well as attacks by Trojans, bombs and plain old operator error. It acquaints you with how to practice safe computing and shows ways of *fighting* viruses instead of just passively worrying about the danger of an intrusion into *your* system.

If you use public domain, freeware, or shareware programs, the chances of attack or infection increases. The obvious answer touted by some writers is never use a public domain or shareware program, and never hook your computer up to the telephone line.

This, despite the very real danger of viruses and other destructive programs, is still poor advice. In my utility directory right now are 314 programs (the result of weeding out hundreds of downloads). There are some real gems in this collection; *useful* programs I got free or for a minimal registration fee that could not otherwise have been bought for any amount of money. Some of them I use every day.

Power Computing

For a commercial program to succeed, it must meet the needs of the widest possible market. Major compromises are made to fit a program within this criteria. Often public domain or shareware programs will better do your specific tasks. These programs also offer features on the leading edge of programming—things the commercial companies, with their much longer development period, will not implement for a year or more.

Pull-down menus, windows, and many other now taken-for-granted features of commercial software first appeared in public domain programs. Of the many thousands of such programs available on Compuserve, Delphi, and the other major computer networks, and on hundreds of local electronic bulletin boards, probably far less than 1 percent are currently infected with a virus, or will cause damage in some other way.

Why let the few sickies who turn out viruses keep you from this power?

Far too many people buy a computer for one particular purpose. Often they purchase just one or two programs and run them all the time. This is akin to owning a 928 Porsche but only using it to drive to the grocery store down the street, never taking it out of first gear.

Computers are performance enhancers. Like the six-gun "equalizer" in the Old West, they are the iron you "pack" to survive in the information age. If you let the threat of viruses scare you away from the networks and bulletin boards, or cause you to shun public domain and shareware, that six-shooter is going to soon *click* empty.

On the other hand, you don't want to sit with your back to the door. Viruses are ornery varmints, but they can be overcome.

Risky Practices

If you ask for trouble, chances are someone, sometime, will oblige you. In fact, these days, it's not necessary to even ask—some worm out there is probably unleashing a new virus as you read this book. Tomorrow, next month, a year from now that virus may mount an assault on the bastions of *your* precious and valuable data.

The first group to start having virus problems were modem junkies—those of us who like to sail the telecommunications sea at night, visiting electronic bulletin boards all over the United States and Canada. With PC Pursuit (a service offered by Telenet), you can make unlimited calls from 6 p.m. to 7 a.m for only $25 total per month. Thousands of boards are now reachable for practically no cost.

A wealth of interesting, usable, and even valuable programs can be quickly accumulated in this way. Unfortunately, viral infection is also spread in the same manner.

Most of the news articles now appearing in your local newspaper from AP or UPI are about virus attacks in large networks of computers such as the Macintoshes at NASA and the EPA, which were infected by the Scores virus, or Lehigh University's virus last year, which hit IBM PCs.

There is a good chance that the initial infection came about because some person with access to the network had downloaded a program on his or her personal computer from a bulletin board somewhere, and then either tried it out at work, or put it on the system in order to share with others.

This is a common practice and, unless a viral infection occurs, a *good* one. The free interchange of information among its employees helps a company or institution become stronger. The better adroit its people are in informational techniques, the more efficient the company or institution.

The problem is that viral infections must be protected against. Computer users in general must have the techniques or software available to them that detects and protects against viruses. More about that in just a bit, but first, what are the risky practices that can result in viral infection?

Here are some practices that *increase* the chance of your

computer system contracting a virus or being otherwise damaged by a Trojan or hacked program:

- Putting a disk of unknown origin into your computer.
- Using other people's disks and programs, and letting them use yours.
- Trading computer programs with strangers, or with people who trade frequently.
- Running a computer program if you're unsure of the following: its origin; the number of times it has been copied; if it has been altered; or what generation copy of the original this one might be.
- Executing *any* new computer program for the first time *without* first making backup copies of every program and data file on your computer.
- Calling another computer using a telephone modem—*especially* a computer of the same type as your own.
- Booting from a floppy disk.
- Hooking your machine into a LAN (Local Area Network).
- Letting *anyone* else put a disk into your machine.
- Using unauthorized copies of commercial software or operating systems.
- Using public domain or shareware programs.

The more of the above that apply to you, the greater the risk of catching a virus. Since most computer users engage in one or more of these activities the real problem is not so much avoiding the chance of infection as *protecting* against infection.

David J. Buerger, in his article "A Specter Is Haunting Networks—The Specter of Viruses, Hidden in Horses" (*InfoWorld*, March 7, 1988), says there is only one sure way to avoid a virus from a program you get from a network. You download only the source code, examine it carefully line by line to "verify the absence of mischievous programmed logic; and then compile the code yourself."

This ultimate precaution could be just as well applied to each and every program obtained for your system, even the ones you buy shrink wrapped off the shelf at the local computer store. But, alas and alack, few of us want to be put to that much bother, even assuming we have the expertise in Pascal and C, which most public domain and shareware programs are written in, or the wide variety of compilers all this code would require.

Buerger also points out the difficult task faced by network system operators in preventing the spread of viruses. The example he gives is that of a virus-infected Macintosh program inadvertently published in Compuserve's *HyperCard* forum. The virus was exterminated in one day but, writes Buerger, 40 people had already unsuspectingly downloaded the program. If the virus program is not caught on a busy day at any major network, several hundred people might have their computers unknowingly contaminated in the course of a year's time, and spread the virus by trading disks with their friends who are not online.

To reiterate, the *real* problem is not avoiding the chance of infection (because that is practically impossible), but *protecting* your system from being infected. Make your computer a wasteland for viruses, full of nothing but shifting sand and the occasional dead cactus. Leave one little oasis of unprotected turf, and the virus will put down roots and bide its time until you make *another* mistake.

How Safe Can You Be? Not Very!

There's a common misconception that if you use only commercial software you'll be sure to avoid infection. Although this practice will lessen the chance of catching a virus, it will not cancel it entirely, as Aldus Corporation recently found out. Aldus has the somewhat dubious distinction of being the first commercial software publisher to inadvertently ship a product with a viral infection.

A March 16, 1988 Associated Press story reported that a virus had gotten into copies of *FreeHand,* a new program that Aldus had just released for Apple Macintosh computers. This was acknowledged by Aldus spokesperson Laury Bryant.

The virus strain involved was one of the supposedly benign ones, the Macintosh Peace virus described in Chapter 1. It was intended to put a message of universal peace on computer screens on March 2, 1988 and then die out.

Software at Aldus was apparently infected when a contractor provided an infected computer training disk to the company. The contractor traced the virus back to a game program obtained from a computer bulletin board. As we discussed earlier, this is a classic way that large computer systems become infected.

Since March, 1988 Aldus has applied stringent virus protection measures. However, the significance of this incident cannot be underrated. Until this incident, it was assumed personal computer viruses only resided in noncommercial software.

Many computer virus "experts" had maintained that the best protection against viruses was to buy all software "off the shelf." Computer store salespeople gleefully echoed this, and totaled up their commissions from extra sales. For, while many $10 or $15 registration-fee shareware might be better than a lot of $99.95 commercial software, who wanted to take the chance of a viral infection? The ease with which the Peace virus invaded Aldus' inhouse system and duplicated software shrink-wrapped for market belied all the experts.

Aldus declined to say how many disks were infected, but as detailed in the AP report, they did admit it was a sizable number. A disk duplicating machine copied the infected *Free-Hand* disks for three days. Half of these had already been distributed to retail outlets when the viral infection was discovered.

Marc Canter, president of MacroMind Inc. of Chicago, was the one who inadvertently passed the virus to Aldus on a training disk. He had been on a trip to Canada when he received an infected program from the Mr. Potato Head game, which is a computerized version of the popular toy.

Unaware of the infection, Canter ran the game once, then used the same computer to work on software for Aldus. The disk he eventually sent to Aldus was infected and the infection spread from it into their system. From there, the virus went out on disks sold to customers and infected their systems, Canter told the AP.

This incident also caused other companies to worry because they also use Canter's services. These clients include such major names as Microsoft, Ashton-Tate, Lotus Development

Corporation, and Apple Computers. Officials at Microsoft, Apple and Lotus all told AP that none of their software was infected, while Ashton-Tate had not replied at the time of these reports.

The Peace virus originated at the Canadian publication *MacMag.* It was distributed by many computer bulletin boards in a program that was supposedly a listing of products made by Apple.

The message in full reads: "Richard Brandow, the publisher of *MacMag,* and its entire staff would like to take this opportunity to convey their universal message of peace to all Macintosh users around the world." A picture of a globe appears below the message.

Brandow said that originally he expected people making unauthorized copies of programs on the machine would spread the virus in the Montreal area and possibly a few other areas of Canada and the United States. However, he said he was shocked later to find that, after the virus program began to appear in the databases of online information services, an estimated 350,000 people in North America and Europe saw the message pop up on their computers on March 2nd, 1988!

Like medical detectives following a chain of biological infections, computer viruses can be traced in the same manner. What computers or disks did the infected computer have contact with? What computers and/or disks did the newly infected carriers come in contact with? This goes on and on, in the manner of ripples spreading out from a pebble tossed in a still pond.

Aldus, a large and respected software manufacturer acted responsibly. They tracked the serial numbers of the product affected by the virus. Those customers received a letter explaining the situation and offering them the opportunity to exchange the disks for free.

Aldus is now taking additional security precautions in the creation, testing, and duplication of all software products. These measures include the use of specific tests and vaccines for known viruses in the market at any given time, and the creation of an isolated secure system for master disk duplication.

"We believe authors of the viruses deserve to be condemned by every member of the Macintosh community. Viruses affect not just Aldus Corporation, but every software company, and potentially every Macintosh owner," said Laury Bryant, Aldus public relations manager. "While we believe that the best insurance against future outbreaks of software viruses is the moral outrage of the Macintosh community, we are also exploring potential legal remedies with our attorneys."

Unlike many viruses, the source of the Peace virus is known. While this virus is apparently benign, it's probably still out there, in hundreds if not thousands of systems.

It's time to hit the main point of this chapter yet again. No matter how assiduously you practice safe computing, in the long run your computer stands a good chance of coming in contact with a virus. The best strategy is to *protect* against infection. Make it impossible for a virus to gain a toehold in your system.

Department of Defense Fights Viruses

Cathryn Conroy, writing in Compuserve's *OnLine Today* for May 18th, 1988 (a service offered on the Compuserve computer network), describes how the Department of Defense is fighting viruses in their systems. Naturally, in the matter of national security, our computerized armed forces have an intense interest in keeping their many computer networks virus-free.

The DOD has instituted procedures to detect and prevent the electronic sabotage. The general concerns of DOD about its computers were reported recently in *Government Computer News*.

"It can spread through computer networks in the same way it spreads through computers," said DOD spokeswoman Sherry Hanson. "The major problem areas are denial of service and compromising data integrity."

Computer scientists at the National Security Agency are in charge of installing hardware and software to prevent viral infection of military systems. The NSA is the largest intelligence agency of the Federal Government and charged with electronic intelligence ranging from vast amounts of cable and radio intercepts to the newer fields of computer communications.

Hanson told *Government Computer News* that DOD is also using specialized ROM devices and intrusion detectors. Because viruses are only a few lines of programming code, they're easy to develop and slip into a system.

After IBM's worldwide internal mail system was infected in December 1987 with an innocent-looking Christmas message that kept duplicating itself many times over (slowing down and even halting the company's massive message system), virus-specialist programmers have installed a filter program that monitors the system and protects from new infections.

As reported in *GCN*, executable programs can't be transferred from one computer to another within IBM's network. Executable programs, of course can serve as Trojan horses to carry viruses from one system to another and, when run, allow the virus to infect new hosts.

Personal Computer Users

Conroy's article continues to relate how personal computer users are also worried. Because a virus remains hidden in a computer's main memory, she writes, and gives the example of a recent Amiga-specific virus which infected almost the entire membership of a Florida Commodore Amiga users group before it was discovered.

The president of the group said he believed the virus originated in Europe on a disk of programs the group received from an overseas source. Like many companies, clubs, institutions, and private individuals, the club now has a checker program to check disks for viruses before they're used.

Al Gengler, a member of the Amiga group, compared the virus to AIDS. "You've got to watch who you compute with now," he said.

In a later *OnLine Today* report by James Moran (May 19), our lawmakers reacted. As might be expected, computer viruses have now come to the attention of Congress and legislators who would like to be assured that U.S. defense computers are safe from viral infections. While defense systems are usually isolated and can't be reached merely by calling via a telephone modem, viruses could enter those systems from an infected disk. After all, even servicepeople play games.

The Defense Authorization Bill for fiscal year 1989 will most likely be concerned with the virus problem. It is expected to direct the Defense Department (DOD) to report on its methods for handling potential viral infections. Congress also wants to know what DOD has done about safeguarding vital military computers. They'd like some assurance that the Defense Department also has considered situations where a primary contractor's computer could be infected and subsequently endanger DOD's own computers (as recently happened to NASA and EPA machines).

Anticipating future hearings, Congressional staffers are soliciting comments from knowledgeable users as to what the report to Congress should cover. Interested parties should forward their comments to Mr. Herb Lin, House Armed Services Committee, 2120 Rayburn House Office Building, Washington D.C. 20515.

Radioactive Viruses?

Computer viruses are scary enough on their own, but how about this? The Nuclear Regulatory Commission announced on August 11, 1988 that it was proposing to fine the Peach Bottom nuclear power plant on the Susquehanna River (near the Pennsylvania-Maryland line) a whopping 1.25 *million* dollars.

This came about after NRC inspectors caught operators numerous times "sleeping and/or other acts of inattention to duty." Sleeping is bad enough when you are supposed to be monitoring a nuclear plant, but it's the "other acts of inattention" that's really more frightening.

They were playing computer games!

One of the classic ways in which large systems receive viral infections, as we discussed earlier, is through people bringing in games downloaded from who knows where. The thought of a virus loose in computers that have anything at all to do with nuclear power plants is very unsettling.

Antiviral Products

A growth industry has sprung up in answer to the virus problem. There are dozens of small startup companies and older already established firms putting out a wide variety of antiviral products.

The Computer Virus Industry Association, while not representing the majority of these companies, is in the lead now in defining standards and terms for such products in the popular and computer press. A July 20, 1988 news release describes the product definitions that members of the association have agreed on.

This standard classification system is for virus protection products and tools. The system was developed to help the public understand the appropriate application of the various tools and to clarify advertising claims.

The Classification system identifies three product groups: Infection Prevention products, Infection Detection products, and Infection Identification products. They are defined as:

Class I	Infection Prevention	This class of product stops the virus replication process and prevents the initial infection from occurring.
Class II	Infection Detection	This class of products detects infection soon after it has occurred and marks the specific components or segments of the system that have become infected.
Class III	Infection Identifications	This class of products identifies specific viral strains on systems that are already infected and removes the virus, returning the system to its state prior to infection.

"The industry anticipates that this standard classification system will assist users in choosing antiviral products that meet the needs of their specific situations," said John McAfee, chairman of the association. "The different product classes address equally different virus problem areas, and a public understanding of these differences is essential."

The Computer Virus Industry Association, the news release continues, is composed of nine major vendors and developers of antiviral hardware and software products. It was formed to address the problems of misleading advertising, the spread of misinformation, and the distribution of ineffective products. The association may be contacted at 4423 Cheeney Street, Santa Clara, California 95054. The phone number is (408) 727-4559.

Prevention Techniques

John McAfee, president of the Computer Virus Industry Association and InterPath Corporation (a manufacturer of antiviral software), offers the following tips on preventing viral infections and the tools with which to fight infections that do occur. Prevention, he says, can be divided into two areas: safe computing practices and antiviral tools.

(Much of the information below is courtesy of InterPath, the Computer Industry Association, and the National BBS Society.)

Approximately 90 percent of all virus infections, or the damaging results of infection, can be easily prevented by implementing the safe usage guidelines below (provided courtesy of InterPath). Most of the other 10 percent of infections, or damaging results, can be avoided by the use of antiviral software or hardware tools.

Here are the recommended safe user practices:

• Never boot from any floppy other than the original write protected disk from the original distribution package! This recommendation is extremely important. Most of the boot sector infector viruses can *only* infect your system if you boot from an infected floppy disk. Booting from borrowed, unknown or multiple disks greatly increases the opportunity for infection.

• One and only one boot disk should be assigned to each and every floppy based PC (systems without a fixed disk), and that disk should be *clearly* labeled as the boot disk for that system.

- If you have a system with a fixed disk, *never* boot from a floppy drive. The only exceptions to this involve recovering from a viral infection as described in the section below.
- Treat public domain and shareware software with caution. Viruses are difficult to detect and usually do not modify the operation of the infected program in any way prior to activation.
- Since a friend or acquaintance might, in good faith, recommend a program that is infected without their knowledge, it's best to limit use of such programs to systems without fixed disks. If you do use them on fixed disks, allocate separate subdirectories for the public domain programs. This will limit exposure since some viruses limit their replication activities to the current subdirectory. You should not place public domain or shareware software in the root directory.
- Create meaningful volume labels on all fixed and floppy disks at format time. Develop a habit of checking volume labels each time a DIR command is executed. Look out for changes in the volume labels.
- Watch for changes in the pattern of your system's activities. Do program loads take longer than normal? Do disk accesses seem excessive for simple tasks? Do unusual error messages occur with regularity? Do access lights on any of the system devices turn on when there should be no activity on that device? Do you have less system memory available than usual? Do programs or files disappear mysteriously? Do you suddenly notice a reduction in available disk space? Any of these signs can be indicative of viral infections.
- If you are in a corporate or multisystem environment, minimize the exchange of executable code between systems wherever feasible. When using resources on someone else's PC (a laser printer, for example), transfer the necessary data on a disk that contains no executable code. Also, do not use disks which are bootable or that contain system files.
- If operating in a network environment, do not place public domain or shareware programs in a common file server directory that could be accessible to any other PC on the network.

- If operating in a network environment, allow no one other than the system administrator to use the file server node.
- If using 3270 emulators connected to mainframe systems, keep all 3270 emulation software together in a separate subdirectory and do not include *any* executable code in the subdirectory that isn't part of the emulator suite. If possible, limit such terminals to 3270 emulation only, and remove all other software from the disk. 3270 emulators are the major gateways through which viruses jump from PCs to mainframes.

Antiviral Tools: Hardware

The use of write-protect tabs is very important in limiting viral spread, and is one of the easiest things you can do. You have most likely bought a box of new, blank disks. In boxes of 5¼-inch disks is a pack of labels and one of small peel-off-stick-on tabs, probably black or silver. On one side of each disk is a small notch called the *write-protect notch*. Placing one of the small tabs over each notch, bending it so it sticks to both sides of the disk and completely covers the hole, prevents the computer from writing (recording) to the disk.

If you use 3½-inch disks, simply slide the write-protect tab found in the upper-right-hand corner of the disk so you can see through the disk. This will prevent the computer from writing (recording) to the disk.

Covering the notch on 5¼-inch disks and sliding the write-protect tab to the open position on 3½-inch disks is similar to punching out the two plastic tongues on the edge of a cassette tape opposite the recording head side—it makes the disk a read-only device to the computer. In other words, neither you nor your computer can accidentally mess it up should some malfunction occur.

All boot floppies (the ones used to initialize your system) should be write-protected as a matter of course. There are also commercial products that will write-protect hard disks, and public domain programs such as WPHD.COM for MS-DOS machines.

Besides using write protection, it's a good habit to remove disks from drive slots and store them away when they're not actually being used. No virus is going to jump out of the computer and get on a disk that's filed away. Obviously, this doesn't hold for a disk inserted in a drive that's just sitting there fat, dumb, and vulnerable.

More complex (and expensive) hardware solutions exist also. Several manufacturers have plug-in boards that provide protection from viral infection, although these are generally more aimed toward overall computer security. However, denying unauthorized access to people also works to some extent against viruses.

Antiviral Tools: Software

Software protection, as defined by the Computer Virus Industry Association, falls into three general categories. These are programs that help prevent the virus from initially infecting your system, programs that detect infection after it has occurred, and programs that identify pre-existing infections. All three types of protection have their strong and weak points.

Later in this book we'll look at specific software packages from the various manufacturers of antiviral products, such as InterPath, the makers of *C-4, Tracer,* and *Detect.* These three products, respectively, fit each of the three categories defined below (and again thanks to John McAfee, President of InterPath, for all of his kind assistance).

Here's an overview of the three types of virus-fighting programs:

Infection Prevention Programs. These programs are TSR (terminate and stay resident) programs that monitor system activity and watch for characteristic viral replication activities. They check all disk I/O and cause a warning to be displayed when unauthorized activities are attempted. Such activities include writes to executable programs, system device drivers, the boot sector, and so forth. They typically redirect the operating system's interrupt vectors and thus intercept requests from all other programs.

This type of protection has the advantage of stopping viruses before they enter the system, thus avoiding the tasks associated with removing viruses. The disadvantage, however, is that viruses can be, and have been, written to avoid detection using this type of system. Also, no software technique can prevent initial infection from a boot sector virus. (This is another reason to follow the above procedures to avoid boot sector infections).

Infection Detection Systems. First, as a note of explanation, these programs only work if the system they're running on *has not been infected* prior to installation. They cannot tell you whether your system has already been infected. They all assume the system is clean.

They work by looking at key information on the system disks (such as file sizes, dates, checksums) and periodically rechecking this information to see if it has changed.

The advantage of this approach is that it's much more difficult for viruses to avoid detection and the technique is therefore much more secure. The disadvantage is that the system must become infected in order to detect the virus. However, if an infection can be identified soon after it occurs, it can be easily removed before it can replicate further and before it has a chance to activate.

Infection Identification Systems. Programs in this category identify specific viruses on systems that are already infected and remove the virus, returning the system to its state prior to infection. This class of products may or may not repair damage done by virus activation. Products in this class may identify only a single virus or multiple types.

The advantage to this class of products is that they can identify pre-existing infection and perform the removal process. The disadvantage is that they work for only a few of the specific viruses and cannot provide general purpose virus protection.

Recovering from a Virus Infection

As might be expected, the procedures needed to recover from an infection are more difficult than initially preventing the infection. However, recovery is possible, usually with a minimum loss of data.

The major concern in recovering from a virus is not just the loss of data (which can be great), but the near certainty of reinfection if the proper procedures aren't followed. Nine out of ten installations that get infected, according to InterPath, suffer a relapse within a week of "cleaning out" the virus. Some organizations have "eradicated" a virus as many as a dozen times, only to have it reoccur shortly after each eradication.

The causes of these reappearances can be traced to two things:

Many viruses do not go away after a warm boot. The Pakistani Brain virus is a good example. In many organizations, the PC is seldom turned off and the prevailing assumption is that a Ctrl-Alt-Del will clean out system memory. This is an incorrect assumption.

Viruses initially infect fixed disk systems by way of a floppy disk. After infection, every floppy that has been placed in the system is also likely to be infected. In large organizations, this can amount to thousands of infected disks that can reinfect systems if not deactivated.

Understanding the above issues goes a long way toward a successful recovery from a virus infection.

The following are the recommended procedures from InterPath and the Computer Virus Industry Association. When an infection is detected, the following procedures should be followed:

1. Determine the extent of the infection. If the virus has not attacked any fixed disks, go to step 12. If the virus has infected the boot sector only, go to addendum.
2. Power down the infected system.
3. Retrieve the original DOS disk from the distribution package. Write-protect it. Place it in the floppy boot drive and power up the system.
4. Ensure that the system has booted properly.
5. Back up all nonexecutable files from all directories onto newly formatted floppy disks or to a tape backup unit. If backing up to another fixed disk, ensure that the disk has not been infected. (If there are any doubts, assume it is infected.) *Do not use the backup utility on the fixed disk.* Use

a utility from the original package. **Note:** At no point in these procedures should you execute *any* program from the infected fixed disk.

6. List all batch files on the infected disk. If any line within any of the batch files seems unusual or unfamiliar do not back up. Otherwise, include the batch files with the backup.
7. Perform a low level format of the infected disk. Recover the initial disk configuration using FDISK and FORMAT.
8. Execute the SYS command for the fixed disk.
9. Restructure your directories.
10. Replace all executable programs from the original distribution packages.
11. Restore the files that were backed up.
12. Locate all floppy disks that may have been inserted in the infected system within the past two years. (We know it sounds extreme, but if this and subsequent steps are not followed, you can be guaranteed to be reinfected within a short period of time.) At your discretion, either destroy them all or continue with the next two steps.
13. Back up all nonexecutable files onto newly formatted floppy disks.
14. Format the suspect disks.

If the virus is a boot sector infector, the recovery process is somewhat simplified. Since boot infectors do not infect executable programs, they can be removed by doing a SYS command on the affected drive. The procedures are:

1. Power down the affected system.
2. Boot from the original DOS write-protected distribution disk.
3. Perform the SYS command on all affected devices.

The above procedures will leave the virus intact on the additional bad sectors originally allocated by the virus, but these viral segments will be deactivated.

Recovery From Trojans, Bombs, and Goof-ups

Viruses are still relatively rare when compared to Trojan programs or bombs which, when run, *immediately* damage your system. First of all, it takes a good deal more programming skills to construct a survivable virus than it does some stupid little program that immediately trashes a disk's file allocation table (FAT).

Remember that a Trojan is simply an attractive utility or some other program that serves as a carrier. The evil secreted inside can be either a virus or a bomb that goes off as soon as the program is run.

Most of the really good programmers, those having the technical know-how and creativity to construct a virus, would consider it *unthinkable* to do so. Programmers are intelligent, likable people for the most part—*good* people who hate the rot of the current virus plague even more than most of us (because they understand the true frightfulness of the ramifications that could be caused by unchecked, widespread viral infection).

Only a very few twisted souls of this elite group create viruses. Hence, the discrete strains of viruses remain moderately small and, so far, infect probably less than 1 percent of IBMs and clones, and Macintoshes. This percentage is even less than that for other brands.

However, this is not so for bombs. We saw in the last chapter that destroying disks, since they are so vulnerable to start with, is easy to do. Any bad kid (as opposed to the many honorable hackers among our youth) can whip up a working bomb in an evening's time and slide it into almost any program. An unhappy employee can leave a cybernetic bomb in his employer's system.

So, your system is more likely to be hit by a Trojan bomb than a virus. One good, *very good*, side effect of most viral protection programs is they will also intercept a bomb's unauthorized attempts at disk access and alert you before damage can occur. They not only protect against intentional destructive efforts, but also against honest mistakes (bugs) in programs and operator error. We all foul up from time to time, and computers can be unforgiving—a viral protection program sometimes gives us a second chance.

One person doing some excellent work in alerting people to Trojans, worms, viruses, and pirated software is Eric Newhouse. Eric electronically publishes *The Dirty Dozen*, a file now found on all the major computer networks and hundreds of local computer bulletin boards.

49

Now in its eighth edition, this online publication explains viruses, Trojans, worms and other such pests. It specifically lists scores of programs known to be "dirty." If you use public domain programs and shareware, it's a very wise precaution to download and check out each new issue of *The Dirty Dozen*, and to support Eric in his work.

Should a Trojan get into your system, Eric Newhouse offers some good tips in recovering from it.

"Perhaps," writes Eric, "your hard disk sounds like a sick moose. Perhaps your drive light starts flashing repeatedly, like a police car's lights. Perhaps your drive just sits in the computer, and the computer doesn't acknowledge its presence."

This has happened to me personally on more than one occasion. There is nothing more frustrating, while fighting a deadline, than having the hard disk go. While sometimes it may be a hardware problem—such as a faulty cable, disk controller, or the hard drive itself—more often the problem is with software. Fixing the hardware costs money, recovering from a software problem, such as one caused by a Trojan, can often be accomplished with only a little effort.

Should you get hit by a Trojan or a bomb (and its going to be pretty obvious that something bad has happened), first remain calm. Try to diagnose the damage and determine if your hard drive was reformatted, the FAT table scrambled, files erased, or the boot sector affected. A Trojan usually does one or more of these four things.

If the Trojan did a low-level format of your hard disk, the only option open is to do a new high-level format and reload your data from your most recent backup. Everything you've done between the time of backup and the bomb hit is gone forever.

Here's an analogy to help you better understand the difference between low- and high-level formats. If you've recorded a cassette tape of, say, 1950s rock songs, you might have labeled it for convenience's sake. The label consists of the title and the counter number so you can fast forward or rewind the tape to the beginning of the wanted song.

If you lay this cassette tape down on a strong magnet, it will be completely erased. This is essentially what low-level formatting does. If, on the other hand, some nerd merely rips off your label, all the songs are still on the tape. It's merely a matter of taking a little time to make a new label. Cleaning off the label is what a high-level format does.

If the Trojan high-level formatted your disk (and this applies to both hard disks and regular floppies), you're in much better shape for recovery of your data. Paul Mace, sometime back, introduced a way to recover data on a disk that had been high-level formatted. Peter Norton and others now offer similar techniques.

The bad news is that most of these format-recovery programs require a snapshot of the disk in order to bring back all the data. This can be an automatic process in your AUTOEXEC.BAT file on IBM PCs and compatibles, or equivalent boot-up programs on other types of computers. You might lose one day's work in this case, but that's much better than two week's worth, or six months' worth.

In the IBM and MS-DOS world, the problem is that the operating system (DOS) fragments large files and sticks parts of them all over the disk to more efficiently fill it. This is mapped out in the FAT (file allocation table) so the file can be found and used in its entirety again. For an "unformatting" program to work, an accurate map of the disk is required, hence the snapshot. Naturally, any file created after this snapshot was taken will be ignored, even though its still on the disk.

Here are three commercial programs that, among many other useful utilities, offer format recovery:

PC-Tools	Central Point, $79.95 retail
Mace+ Utilities	Paul Mace $99.95 retail
Advanced Norton Utilities	Peter Norton, $150.00 retail

While these types of utilities may sound expensive, one recovery can more than pay for them. How much is your time worth?

If the Trojan scrambled your FAT table and left the rest of the disk intact, you would have recovery options also. Remember that the FAT is the map for the operating system to find all parts of a file—this map has to be reconstructed.

The best way to reconstruct is to keep constant backups of

the FAT table using Norton's or *PC-Tools,* or a public domain
program such as FATBACK.COM. If you can't simply recopy
the FAT back to the hard disk, you'll have to painstakingly use
a sector editor, like those included in the *Norton Utilities, PC-
Tools* and lots of other popular utility packages.

Sector editors will allow experienced users to reconstruct
their FAT from the garbage now in its place. This type of recovery does require more than a little knowledge of your computer
operating system's disk structure.

Undeleting Files

The situation of erased files is the easiest to recover from (and
something you should know just for files deleted by mistake).
Lots of commercial and public domain packages are available
that *undelete* deleted files.

The *Norton Utilities, PC-Tools, MACE+*, and *UNDEL.
COM* (a public domain program) will all accomplish undelete
files for you. The commercial products are somewhat more reliable in undeleting and are obviously more expensive.

You should always undelete your most recent files first.
Since the operating system (DOS) fragments files to fill all
available space, older erased files (which are now invisible to
DOS) may have segments already overwritten.

The first sector on a hard disk (and a floppy) is called the
boot sector. This contains the necessary information for the
computer to initialize itself. Not too long ago, the boot sector
on my own system was overwritten. All my files were still
there, but the computer simply would not boot—responding
only with a Probable Non-DOS Disk error message. It wound
up costing me several hours to back up the files on the disk, reformat it with new system files, and reload the backup.

In this case, it was not a Trojan or virus that caused the
problem. I do a lot of reviews and books about various programs. Some companies are kind enough to send me pre-re-
lease versions so I get a head start in doing a book on their
product. One of these versions had a bug in it (long since
fixed), but it did cause me some hassle at a time when I had
several deadlines to meet.

If the boot sector on your hard disk should get erased or written over, there are four things to do. Before you do them, however, if you don't have a current backup of the disk, make one *now*. There is the possibility that you might have to destroy some files to restore your hard disk to boot status. With a good backup, you can then load these files back in place.

First, attempt to restore the system to the disk. On MS-DOS disks, these include two hidden files as well as COMMAND.COM. To do so, insert the floppy disk that came with your computer that has SYS.COM on it. Using the syntax SYS C: for a hard disk (or SYS A: for a floppy) will transfer these system files to the hard disk (*maybe*).

If the system did transfer (you got no error message), copy COMMAND.COM back onto the hard drive. If the hard drive still won't boot, try the next remedy.

Should you have the *MACE+* utilities from Paul Mace, go to the "other utilities" section and "restore boot sector." If you have installed and have been using *MACE+* correctly, this will cure your problem.

If none of the above works *do a complete backup of the disk* (if you haven't already done it). Now you're going to have to do a low-level format of the hard disk. Instructions on how to do this depends on which controller card you have. This information should have come with your hard disk controller card.

It's important to map out bad sectors (which all hard disks have) using a program for that purpose (Eric Newhouse recommends SCAV.COM by Chris Dunford) or by manually entering the locations of bad sectors into the low-level format program. After the low-level format, run the utility FDISK.COM (it comes with DOS) to create a DOS partition. You can use your DOS manual for help in using FDISK.

Once this low-level format is finished, you'll have to do a *high-level* format on your hard disk (yes, Trojans are a nuisance, aren't they?). Do this by putting your original DOS disk (the one that came with the computer) in drive A: and type *FORMAT <drive letter>:/S/V*. <Drive letter> represents the letter of the disk you're formatting. This formats the disk, putting the necessary DOS system files on it and verifying that the copy is exact.

Try rebooting again.

Should things still be fouled, you'll have to find a professional computer repairperson to fix your drive or accept the fact that the drive cannot be booted. I recommend strongly against the latter—having to boot from a floppy increases the chances of viral infections.

5
HOW THE EXPERTS DEAL WITH VIRUSES

All the wit in the world is not in one head.

Old Proverb

The computer virus problem is both old and new. It is (at least theoretically) as old as computers themselves, but *new* to the general public. Because computers—thanks to immense drops in prices and incredible increases in unit production in the last few years—are now in so many more hands, viruses now can affect large numbers of people instead of just a few companies or institutions. Virus stories are in the newspapers almost weekly now, and they've been featured on national news broadcasts.

With actual virus infections and, even more importantly, the *threat* of infection, a wide spectrum of system managers, programmers, and others in the computer industry have been forced to become experts on viruses.

Computer viruses are still, for most, a relatively new problem. This holds true for the majority of the computer industry as well. In the process of researching this book, we've found that some very good people are devising ways to detect and protect against viruses.

This chapter is a brief look at just a few people on the "front lines" and how they're leading the fight against computer viruses. We regret that lack of space doesn't allow us to include everyone spoken to. While the virus problem is not yet as severe as it could very easily get, the future of the Information Age might well depend on people like those quoted below. They are soldiers in the war to preserve data.

Ross Greenberg: A *Flu_Shot* Against Viruses

According to Steve Gibson, writing in his "Tech Talk" column in the computer industry weekly newspaper, *InfoWorld*, one of the most effective virus protection programs available is also one of the least expensive: *Flu_Shot+*, by Ross Greenberg (the product is reviewed later in this book). A software author and nationally recognized virus expert and consultant, Greenberg lives in New York City and runs his own company, Software Concepts Design.

Ross has been very gracious in providing both information and additional contacts for this book. The interview below came from comments Ross made to the author over the phone, from a Round Table conference on GEnie, and extracts from *Flu_Shot+*'s documentation. All are combined and reproduced here through his kind consent.

"The right to use *Flu_Shot+*," Ross said, in explaining the shareware concept under which his viral-protection product is marketed, "is contingent upon your paying for the right to use it. I ask for ten dollars as a registration fee. This entitles you to get the next update shipped to you when available, and allows you to pay me, in part, for my labor in creating the entire Flu_Shot series. I don't expect to get my normal consulting rate or to get a return equal to that of other programs which I've developed and sell through more traditional channels. That's not my intent, or I would have made *Flu_Shot+* a commercial program and you'd be paying lots more money for it.

"Some people are uncomfortable with the shareware concept, or believe there's no such thing as Trojan or Virus programs, and that a person who profits from the distribution of a program such as Flu_Shot must be in it for the money. I've created an alternative for these folks. I'll call it 'charityware.' You can also register *Flu_Shot+* by sending me a check for

$10 made out to your favorite charity. Be sure to include a stamped and addressed envelope. I'll forward the money on to them and register you fully."

Ross Greenberg has been involved with the computer virus problem since the current scare first came to the public's attention.

"When Flu_Shot came out, and the news of viruses first hit the media," he said, "I was getting about 40 calls a day on the average. These were from people who were totally convinced they were infected. Of those people, I'd say that no more than five calls per day were legitimate viruses. Obviously those people had been hit bad. They usually called me up because they had Flu_Shot but had not installed it yet. They figured they'd try one more piece of software out and *boom*, they got hit."

A Trojan, Ross explains, is a program which does something other than that which you intended it to do. A virus, by that definition *is* a Trojan. The main difference is a virus will infect other programs with a copy of itself, and later will turn "normal" Trojan on you. This implies that the virus is a far more dangerous case of being "Trojaned."

The normal Trojan, when it goes off, will only erase or damage the data on whatever disks are currently available to it. The virus allows for the Trojan to be transmitted to other disks, and therefore other computers. Additionally, an infected program can lay dormant until you run it at some later time. The virus hangs out, waiting to be executed and will eventually "go off" causing a bit of havoc on your all important data.

"In Flu_Shot," he said, "I've attempted to make the program only advise you of suspicious operations as they occur. You are then given the choice of allowing the operation to continue, allowing *all* operations to continue until the program ends, or aborting the operation. This allows you to run programs such as DOS's own FORMAT program and allows it to continue to operate normally, but advises you of potentially dangerous operations which normally shouldn't happen. You don't expect, for example, a FORMAT operation to take place when you're using that spiffy new checkbook balancing program.

"These days, anybody who wants to be protected can be with Flu_Shot on the el cheapo, so many people are being protected. Plus, a lot of bulletin board operators out there are much more cautious now. However, there are a few bulletin boards I know of where the sysop does nothing but make them available to you. Unfortunately my own computer club board does this. I had to fight them tooth and nail to get Flu_Shot on there.

"For the most part, bulletin board operators and most users are much more cautious overall now. The people who are getting hit the hardest these days I would say are probably universities—for a whole variety of reasons.

"Some of the large corporate structures are being hit, but not that badly. Obviously if you hit a GE with 40,000 PCs, that's going to do considerably more damage than if you hit Fred's computer in the other room. Of course, you won't hear anything from the folks at big companies if they get hit. They might call me up and say 'Hi, we're infected, but don't tell anybody. What do we do?' And a couple of very large corporations have called me up and said 'Hi, we're infected, but don't tell anybody. What do we do?'"

Ross then made a very important point about virus infections:

"The thing to remember," he said, "is right now it's summer. A lot of those university students are probably at home now concocting their favorite viruses. So when they come back in September, I suspect there will be an increase in infections. It's a nice, interesting, fun hobby for some people.

"Given that, I expect us to have more virus hits in September and October. Additionally, I'm a little worried about virus infections in general. Right now, programs like Flu_Shot or any one of the others, they do everything they can to protect against viruses. There's no virus that I know of which currently gets around Flu_Shot. Yet, if I wanted to, I could write one tomorrow that would get around every single piece of software out there, including Flu_Shot.

"Writing a virus to attack an unprotected system is really easy. On a protected system, however—with Flu_Shot or Vaccine or one of the others—writing a virus is much more difficult. The folks who are capable of getting around Flu—Shot or whatever else are not typically the virus-writer type.

"No one has been caught that I'm aware of. I'm not certain, actually, of what crime they could be prosecuted under. Assumption: If one were caught, the authorities would nail them on some seemingly weird charge, such as 'malicious mischief' and then they'd get huge fines, a reasonable jail sentence, and all of their equipment would be confiscated. Remember also that 'breaking' into a government computer system is a federal offense of pretty serious merit. I would assume that the first time your local Congressman lost his re-election data, well, they'd be pretty angry and some laws would be changed pretty quickly.

"Getting back to your point, it's impossible to say how many computers are infected. I am just going to pick a guess here. I think nationwide 10,000 people."

Since computer filing systems are so vulnerable (see Chapter 3: How Viruses Work), we asked Ross his opinion on whether computer manufacturers would move soon to make their equipment more resistant to infection.

"I doubt it," he said. "First, to my knowledge, with the exception of Apple, none of the major manufacturers have yet come out and said that there are viruses. No one has said 'We are doing something about it.' Apple said, 'Well, here's something to make you feel better.'"

Ross is referring here to the Virus RX program released at the end of April by Apple Computer. This free antiviral program was created to answer the Scores virus infection in Macintosh computers (see "The Scores Virus" in Chapter 2). The program is available at no charge through Apple dealers and on various computer bulletin boards, and will be covered in greater detail later in this book.

"Operating systems," Ross continued, "like OS/2 as an example, now do have a protection mechanism to prevent a virus from spreading. Are they currently effective? Yes. But, while these techniques do fight against viruses, they are just the natural progression of filing systems rather than specific virus-protection design on the part of manufacturers."

Some programmers are beginning to include virus protection routines in their application programs. Ross Greenberg has also done this, especially in his commercial product, *RamNet* (a powerful background, memory resident communications program that enables you to run a bulletin board, upload and download, or complete a wide range of other tasks automatically in the background while using other programs in the foreground).

"Yes," he said, "*RamNet* had that from day one. But it originally wasn't for viruses but to make sure no one was tapping the code. Such techniques are easy in .COM programs, but very difficult to do with .EXE programs.

"I guess most of the people out there have a simple question: Do viruses exist, and how common are they? Additionally people are concerned about what their chances are of picking one up off of their local BBS or from CompuServe, GEnie, or BIX.

"Well, they do exist. I have about 20 viruses in 'quarantine' on my BBS machine. The odds of you picking one up on a service like GEnie is pretty slim, though. Their files are checked and rechecked, and then verified to make sure they're as safe as possible.

"Does this mean that you can't get one at all? No. I have one virus here which is 'set to go off' in September. Another one waits for your disk to get over 90 percent full. So, the problem *does* exist. Your odds of getting one, though, is about the same as the odds of you getting a laced Tylenol capsule.

"My *Flu_Shot+* program attempts to thwart the attempts of the virus program. It tries to intercept any of the 'normal' things a virus would do, including direct disk writes, and changes to any type of .COM or .EXE program.

"I am specifically *not* in the business of protecting people. Flu_Shot has drained a lot of my resources from my normal business. I get about 30 calls per day regarding viruses and Trojans. That is time I can't give to my normal customer base. Now, I created Flu_Shot to help people who can't protect themselves. I felt that putting it out as a $10 shareware product would allow me to pay for distribution, maybe pay for a new phone line, and otherwise allow me to break even. I love this silly little field of ours, and feel privileged to get paid to do work I enjoy.

"The little worms who write viruses are hurting the field I love. Hence, I desire to make them extinct. As to publicity: The amount of publicity that the whole virus question generates is a feedback loop. I'm more than a little embarrassed that the normal, noncomputer media reported on the virus problem long before the computer press did. However, this is a subject which has to be reported on, just as the Tylenol problem had to be reported on. The Tylenol problem changed society a small amount. The virus problem will change computer society a little. But, I tend to think that the vehement disgust of people such as you and I is going to turn the little worms off. If they wanted favorable opinion, they sure are *not* getting it! Hence, the publicity is, in my opinion, not a bad thing. You're now all aware of the problem, which I've known about for three years!

Protecting Yourself

Ross offers the following suggestions on how you can protect your system against viral infection.

"After you make a backup, you might want to consider using one of the myriad vaccine programs out there. I'm biased, and like Flu_Shot, but some of the others are quite good as well.

"You want to be certain that your data is secure. Programs you can always replace with the distribution copy. Aside from that, know where you get your programs from. Although a shrink-wrap is not a guarantee that your program is uninfected, it's a 99.999 percent guarantee.

"If you use PD software, make sure that the BBS you get it from has checked it out. I know that the managers on GEnie spend a great deal of time insuring their own public domain library, and that other commercial services do as well.

"Remember that people who log onto GEnie and the other national services are all verified, and have their credit card information on file. So, it would be rare for someone to even try to pass a Trojan or a virus intentionally. The same cannot be said of many BBS systems who allow you to download from the new uploads section immediately after a program is posted. Ask your sysop if they check out the code. If the answer is 'No,' get it from someplace else.

"Viruses can infect any program that is executed. They can infect device drivers (the SYS files in your root directory), and can infect the boot sector as well. As such, these 'nonspecific' viruses can infect an entire disk pretty quickly, and are the most dangerous ones. Making a file read-only is done through a normal DOS call. Any program can change the attributes easily, then change them back if it wishes. Finally, just as you can get a directory listing, a program can as well and can put out a call for all files matching a pattern, such as *.COM, or *.EXE.

"Think of what you can do from the command line. You type DIR C:*.COM from the A: drive, and you find the COM files on C:. A Virus or Trojan can exploit the DOS system conventions just as easily. Some of the older monochrome monitors could be burned out by a program, but I've not seen a virus which does this.

"As for sysops who are nonprogrammers: Make a full system backup, close the system down, test out the code, then release only the tested code. Try checksumming *every* file on the disk, then comparing it after you test out the newly uploaded code.

"The *Dirty Dozen* list is a *great* list! But, remember that *any* program can contain a virus. An upload of your favorite PD program could (potentially) have a virus in it. That's why testing, such as GEnie does, is so important. Trojans, since they don't spread, will eventually end up on the DD list, so it is extraordinarily valuable in that regard."

Ross was then asked about the names of known viruses.

"Well, I don't give the little suckers names! I have about 20 viruses that have been uploaded to my board (remember that I actually *ask* for them, so that isn't a normal number we're speaking of). *Flu_Shot+* does work against the Brain virus, though. A virus (or a Trojan) is only dangerous when it is run. You can safely examine the program you suspect of containing a virus, including deARCing it. Only when you execute a program does it get tricky.

"My favorite virus was one which went TSR (Terminate

and Stay Resident), and attached itself onto the timer tick. Once per minute it would examine the screen and search out four consecutive numbers. When it found a set, it would randomly transpose two of them. Sounds cute, but could be dangerous if you're using *Lotus 1-2-3* to run a multimillion dollar company!

"Your BIOS is in two parts. One, in ROM, can't be changed except by physically pulling the chip. The second part is stored on disk, as a hidden file, and is called IBMBIO on IBM-DOS, IOSYS on MS-DOS. That *can* be changed and can be infected. The other part of your configuration is in CMOS RAM, that is, battery backed up RAM. It can be modified by a virus, but isn't really dangerous. *Flu—Shot+* tries to protect against that particular change. Alas, that's been a problem spot (read that as 'bug!') in Flu—Shot for longer than I like to admit. Copy-protected software can be a problem if it gets infected. My suggestion: Call up the manufacturer and ask them what *they* intend to do about it!"

Ross Greenberg's virus protection program, *Flu—Shot+* will be reviewed later in the book. It's a shareware program, meaning that you'll find it on many computer networks and bulletins boards. You can download it and try it free—paying the $10 registration fee only if you decide that the program is worthwhile for you.

"Copies which you download from the RamNet BBS (212-889-6438)," Ross said, "or from the NYACC BBS (718-539-3338), BIX, COMPUSERVE, DELPHI, GEnie or from USENET are all good clean copies.

"Copies from most BBS's are going to be clean, too. I suggest that you do not use a copy unless the sysop of the BBS states that he or she has tried out the uploaded copy and proclaims it not to be Trojaned or wormed in any way. I do expect that some worm out there, disappointed at my attempts to remove what little joy they get out of life will attempt to use the popularity of *Flu Shot+* in some way to further spread the disease in his or her mind."

You may also order a copy direct from Greenberg by sending $10 to Software Concepts Design, 594 Third Avenue, New York, New York 10016.

Reward Offered

There is one additional service Ross Greenberg is doing for the computer industry. He is offering *rewards* for anyone turning in someone who has deliberately spread viral infection. This worthwhile effort should be supported. Below is the text of his reward offer:

*   *   *

Somebody out there knows who the worms are. Even they must have someone who is a friend. True, I can't think of any reason someone would befriend a worm, but somebody who doesn't know better has. Well, I'm offering a reward for the capture and conviction of these worms. Enough already with software protection schemes, hardware protection schemes, or any protection at all. It shouldn't be required!

Here's the deal: If you're a software or hardware manufacturer, or you have some software or hardware you don't need, consider donating it to this worthy cause. I don't know what the legal and tax ramifications of that donation would be. I'm not a lawyer and we can cross that bridge when we get to it (donations are not sent unless a person actually qualifies to receive them).

Anyway, if you know one of these worms, turn them in! Call me up, send me a letter, a telegram, or leave a message for me on my BBS. Indicate who you *know* is worming about. I'll keep your name confidential. It is surprisingly easy to get the authorities in on this—they're as concerned about what is happening to our community as we are. I'll presume that they'll end up putting a data tap on the phone line of the accused worm. Then, when he next uploads a Trojan or a virus to a BBS, he'll get nailed. The authorities are pretty good about this stuff: They'll not tap a phone or take any action whatsoever without adequate proof.

Will your dropping a dime on this worm be adequate proof? I don't know. Again, a bridge to cross when we approach it. However, assuming that this slimeball gets nailed, you'll get all of the software and hardware other people have donated. You'll also get the satisfaction of knowing you've done a good thing—you've helped an industry and community continue to grow. This *is* your community, and the vast majority of people in it are good people who shouldn't have to fear others. Your friend is not really a friend; he uses you to justify his own existence. When people use you like that, they're not friends; they're leeches. And you've probably got better things to do than let others use you like that. Most importantly, the worm out there won't know if one of his friends has already turned him in, so he won't know if his phone is tapped.

If *I* were a worm, and considering what kind of friends I would have, I'd be sure that somebody dropped a dime on me. And therefore intelligent worms (perhaps I'm giving them too much credit?) must presume that their lines are tapped and that they're gonna go to jail if they continue what they're doing. So just stop, you miserable little lowlifes, huh? You're going to be arrested. You're going to have to put up with indignities which even you don't deserve! Your equipment will be confiscated. You'll never get a job in the industry. You're going to go to jail. All this will happen because one of your friends actually has a conscience and knows what's right and what's wrong. And what you're doing is wrong.

So, let me get back to the kind of programming I enjoy—productive programming. And turn your programming to useful, interesting, and productive programming. You have the talent to do something useful and good with your life. What you're doing is hurting the industry and hurting the community that would welcome someone with your talents with open arms. The satisfaction of helping far surpasses the satisfaction you must get from hurting innocent people. So just stop.

Sincerely, Ross M. Greenberg

*   *   *

A registration form for pledging software or hardware to the reward fund is included in the archive of *Flu_Shot+*, which is available from all the major computer networks or from Mr. Greenberg's own board (see below).

Ross Greenberg may be contacted at Software Concepts Design, 594 Third Avenue, New York, New York 10016 or phone 1-212-889-6431 between 9:00 a.m. and 5:00 p.m., Eastern Time. Ross also provides a 24-hour per day computer bulletin board with virus information. Use 1200 or 2400 baud, no parity, 8 bits, 1 stop bit (8N1) and call 1-212-889-6438. He also may be contacted via MCI Mail and on BIX as 'greenber' and on CompuServe/PCMagNet as 72241,36.

Raymond M. Glath: Keeping Watch for Viruses

Ray Glath is president of RG Software Systems (2300 Computer Avenue, Suite I-51, Willow Grove PA 19090 or call 1-215-659-5300). His company's virus protection product, *Disk Watcher,* is reviewed later in this book. The firm also manufactures the *PC Tracker* microcomputer inventory and management system used by many large companies. This interview contains material from a phone conversation and from documentation supplied, courtesy of Mr. Glath.

"Many who create virus programs view them as a joke," Ray Glath said, "but even nondestructive viruses, like ones that display 'gotcha' messages on a screen, cost a business time, money, and morale. We think our simple pop-up warning of unusual activity happening in a system can save incalculable headaches."

RG Software Systems, Glath continued, now offers a white paper that details its rational view of computer viruses and explains countermeasures that won't limit access to shareware, online services, electronic mail, or user groups. The paper outlines steps that Information Center managers, MIS/DP groups, and office managers should take immediately to avoid viral infection and lost productivity caused by disk-borne computer virus, time-bomb, and "Trojan horse" programs. The free white paper, available by request on company letterhead, provides practical solutions business users can implement quickly without sacrificing system flexibility.

"So far," Ray said, "viruses are better publicized in the academic environment, but they're spreading among businesses. Smart companies are taking steps to guard against them.

"Several attacks have been documented by the press and, from firsthand experience, I can attest to the fact that those reported do exist. We have seen them and successfully tested our Disk Watcher product against them. Reputable individuals have reported additional viruses to us, but these have not reached the scale of distribution achieved by the now infamous 'Lehigh,' 'Brain,' 'Israeli,' and 'Macintosh' viruses.

"We do expect the situation to worsen due to the attention it's received. Taking simple lessons from history, a new phenomenon, once given attention, will be replicated by individuals who otherwise have no opportunity for personal attention.

"Now that there are products for defense from viruses, the virus writers have been given a challenge; and for those people who have always wanted to anonymously strike out at someone but didn't know of a method to do so, the coverage has provided a 'How To' guide."

Glath then addressed the problem of distinguishing a bug or hardware malfunction from a true virus.

"This can be a tough one. With the publicity surrounding viruses, many people are ready to believe that any strange occurrence while computing may have been caused by a virus, when it could simply be an operational error, hardware component failure, or a software bug.

"While most commercial software developers test their products exhaustively. There is always the possibility that some combination of hardware, mix of installed TSRs, user actions, or slight incompatibilities with compatible or clone machines or components can cause a problem to surface."

Glath recommends that you remember the following key points:

1. Examine the probabilities of your having contacted a virus.

2. Don't just assume that you've been attacked by a virus and abandon your normal troubleshooting techniques or those recommended by the product manufacturer.
3. When in doubt contact your supplier or the manufacturer for tech support.
4. Having an effective "Virus Protection" system installed may help you determine the cause of the problem.

Protection from Viruses

Do you need some form of protection from viruses?

"It wouldn't hurt," Glath said. "You do lock the door to your home when you go out, right?

"Plan in advance the methods you'll use to ward off virus attacks. It's a far more effective use of management time to establish preventive measures in a calm environment instead of making panic decisions after a virus attack has occurred."

Can you be absolutely safe?

"No! Any security system can be broken by someone dedicated and knowledgeable enough to put forth the effort to break the system."

How can a software product protect against viruses?

"There are several approaches that have been developed.

"One form is an 'inoculation' or 'signature' process whereby the key files on a disk are marked in a special way and periodically checked to see if the files have been changed. Depending on the way in which this is implemented, this method can actually interfere with programs that have built-in integrity checks.

"Another method is to write protect specific key areas of the disk so that no software is permitted to change the data in those places.

"We at RG Software Systems believe that preventive measures are the most effective. The Disk Watch system provides multiple lines of defense:

"A batch type program automatically checks all active disk drives for the presence of certain hidden virus characteristics when the computer is started, and a TSR (Terminate and Stay Resident) program monitors ongoing disk activity throughout all processing. The batch program can also be run on demand at any time to check the disk in a specific drive.

"The TSR program, in addition to its other 'Disaster Prevention' features, contains a series of proprietary algorithms that detect the behavior characteristics of a myriad of virus programs and yet produce minimal overhead in processing time and 'false alarm' reports. *Disk Watcher* is uniquely able to tell the difference between legitimate IP activity and the IO activity of a virus program.

"When an action occurs indicative of a virus attempting to reproduce itself, alter another program, set itself up to be automatically run the next time the system is started or attempting to perform a massively damaging act, *Disk Watcher* will automatically pop up. The user will then have several options, one of which is to immediately stop the computer before any damage can be done. Detection occurs *before* the action takes place. Other options allow the user to tell *Disk Watcher* to continue the application program and remember that this program is permitted to perform the action that triggered the pop-up."

Choosing a Virus Protection Package

Mr. Glath then provided some tips on how to choose the best virus protection package for you.

"Since the first reports of virus attacks appeared in the press, a number of virus prevention products have quickly appeared on the market, produced by companies wishing to take advantage of a unique market opportunity. This is to be expected. We are one of them with our *Disk Watcher* product.

"It should be pointed out, however, that only a few months have transpired since the first major media stories started appearing.

"Those companies that have had to build a product from scratch during this limited amount of time have had to design the defensive system, write the program code, write the user's manual, design the packaging, Alpha test, Beta test, and bring their product through manufacturing to market. A monumental task in a miraculously short period of time.

"Companies that have had products on the market that include virus protection, or products that were enhanced to include virus protection, such as *Disk Watcher,* have had extra time and field experience for the stabilization of their products.

"As a professional in this industry, I sincerely hope that the quickly developed products are stable in their released form."

Glath suggests the following evaluation points be applied as a standard for all types of software products:

• Price
• Performance
• Ease of Use
• Ease of Learning
• Ease of Installation
• Documentation
• Copy Protection
• Support

"A virus protection package, like a security system for your home, requires a close scrutiny. You want the system to do the job unobtrusively and yet be effective."

Special Considerations for Virus Protection Packages

Ray Glath of RG Software Systems provides the following list of twelve special considerations in choosing a virus protection package:

Amount of impact the package may have on your computer's performance. If the package is RAM Resident, does it noticeably slow down your machine's operations? If so, with what type of operation? Are program startups slowed? Are database operations slowed?

Level of dependency on operator intervention. Does the package require the operator to perform certain tasks on a regular basis in order for it to be effective? (Such as only checking for virus conditions on command). Does the package require much time to install and keep operation? For example, must the protection package be used each time new software is installed on the system?

Impact on productivity . . . Annoyance level. Does the package periodically stop processing and/or require the operator to take some action? If so, does the package have any capability to learn its environment and stop its interference?

False alarms. How does the package handle situations that appear to be viruses, but are legitimate actions made by legitimate programs? Are there situations where legitimate jobs will have to be rerun or the system rebooted because of the protection package? How frequently will this occur? How much additional end-user support will the package require?

The probability the package will remain in use? Will there be any interference or usage requirements that will discourage the user from keeping the package active? (It won't be effective if they quickly desire to de-install it and perhaps only pretend they are using it when management is present.)

Level of effectiveness it provides in combating viruses. Will it be effective against viruses produced by individuals in the following experience levels?

Level 1—Typical End User (Basic knowledge of using applications and DOS commands.)

Level 2—Power User (Knowledge of DOS command processor, hardware functions, BASIC programming, and other advanced features.)

Level 3—Applications Programmer (Knowledge of programming languages and DOS service calls.)

Level 4—Systems Engineer (Knowledge of DOS and Hardware internal functions.)

Level 5—Computer Science Professor who develops viruses for research purposes.

Which types of viruses intrusion will it be effective against? Covert Entry? Overt Entry?

Does it detect a virus attempting to spread or clone itself?

Does it detect a virus attempting to place itself into a position to be automatically run?

If a virus gets into the computer, which types of virus damage will it detect: Massive Destruction? Partial Destruction? Selective Destruction? Random Havoc Destruction? Annoyance?

Does the software detect a virus before or after it has infected a program or made its attack?

Does the publisher claim total protection from all viruses?

Does the software provide any assistance for post mortem analysis of suspected problems? If a virus symptom is detected and the computer is brought to a halt, is there any supporting information for analyzing the problem other than the operator's recall of events?

Impact on your machine's resources. How much RAM is used? Is any special hardware required?

Is the product compatible with your hardware configuration? Your operating system version? Your network? Other software you use, especially TSRs?

Can the package be used by current computing personnel without substantial training? What type of computing experience is required to install the package?

Background of the publisher. References. Who is using this or other products from this publisher? How is this company perceived by its customers? The press? How long has the publisher been in business?

Was the product Beta tested? By valid, well-known organizations or by friends of the company's owner? Was the product tested against any known viruses? Successfully?

What about ongoing support? In what form? At what cost? Does the company plan to upgrade its product periodically? What is the upgrade policy? Expected costs?

Does the package provide any other useful benefits to the user besides virus protection?

From the Oracles at Delphi

One of the large public worldwide computer services is Delphi. Located in Cambridge, Massachusetts, Delphi has local telephone number access throughout the United States and Canada. In the various special interest groups of Delphi are many thousands of public domain and shareware programs for downloading. The author of this book (whose user name on Delphi is also AUTHOR) manages the Writers Group, which has several hundred available programs just by itself.

There are special interest groups for the various types of computers, and groups for hobbies, science fiction, theology, business, games, and others. Each of these groups has a database section that offers programs.

Like all the other major networks, Delphi management in general and various sysops in particular are concerned with preventing viral infection in the programs provided to users. While it is impossible for *any* network to fully guarantee that no virus-infected program will ever slip through, Delphi has been one of the leaders in protecting its users.

Jeff Shulman and the Macintosh

Jeff Shulman, the new ICONtact Manager (Delphi's Macintosh-oriented special interest group) is one of the sysops concerned with preventing virus infections. In fact, he is the author of a virus detection program for the Macintosh. He was also the first person to inform Aldus that their *FreeHand* program was being distributed with the Peace virus.

"When viruses first appeared on the Mac," Jeff said, "I, too, wondered how to protect Delphi users from downloading an infected file. Using tools like *ResEdit* to examine each file was an extremely time consuming process. What I needed was a tool that could quickly scan files for the various 'tags' viruses left in files. This utility should also be easily modifiable should new strains of viruses come along.

"That was how *VirusDetective*™ was born. *VirusDetective* (VD) was written as a DA so it could be run at any time from any program (like immediately after I download a file). What VD does is search through all the files in a given folder, recursively (or the entire disk) looking for files that meet its matching criteria. Here is where I used my knowledge of Mac programming (I have several programs on the market, like *FontDisplay, DiskLock* and *WriteFontSize*) and how viruses work to come up with a list of programmable search criteria.

"VD can be configured to select a file by its type, creator, or by looking for specific resources. The resources may be searched for by name, ID, type, size, or size range. Once a file is found that matches its search criteria, it tells the user and gives him a chance to remove that particular resource.

"Now, most viruses in the Mac world *cannot* be *fully* eradicated by removing a single resource. VD's main purpose is virus detection, not eradication. There are several other programs that are built to eradicate specific viruses. VD also does not search for suspect viruses like *Interferon* does. You must tell VD exactly what to look for. Thus, it *is* possible for a new virus to sneak by VD (as well as the other programs).

"However, in the highly connected Mac community, it will quickly be identified. Once identified, VD can easily be reconfigured by the user to also include that virus in its search criteria. The other detection programs may require reprogramming and redownloading to include a new virus.

"VD is being marketed as shareware. It has had little return so far. This is probably due in part to the fact the other programs are free.

"Another feature of VD is its ability to keep a log of all the files searched and those that matched the search criteria. It's this logging capability and the ability to easily configure the search criteria that enables VD to search for just about anything and not *just* for viruses.

"I also use CE Software's *Vaccine INIT* and run every program posted before it is released. That way, should a new unknown virus pass VD's testing, hopefully, Vaccine would pick it up. I'm also extra careful with postings from new uploaders and people whose names I don't recognize. A majority of the stuff I cross-post from the noncommercial networks is also checked by those moderators.

"I'm not saying that a virus infected program will never be posted. Just as the virus scare started, all three major networks did have a virus program up on the board but it was *quickly* detected and removed with 24 hours on all the services. I regularly read messages from both CIS and GEnie as well as Usenet and INFO-MAC. Between all five networks, Mac viruses are caught and removed before they have a chance to spread.

"My advice to someone who wants to be extra careful is to not download any new file when it first comes out but to wait a week. Unless it is a *very* clever virus with a long time delay, it will be found out and removed in the week's time.

"The telecommunicating Mac community is *very* large and *very* quick at finding these things out."

Marty Goodman of Delphi

Marty Goodman is SIGOP for Delphi's CoCo Sig, and also is involved with the OS9 and Portable Place groups as well.

"The Radio Shack color computer," Marty said, "is operated under one of two operating systems: RS DOS (otherwise known as DISK EXTENDED COLOR BASIC) and OS9.

"Now, RS DOS is a ROM-based operating system and so is totally, utterly, and completely invulnerable to any possible virus by virtue of its existing *only* as unalterable firmware. This takes care of the majority of Color Computer users.

"The more advanced minority who use OS9 use a UNIX-like operating system. (Described by *Dr. Dobbs Journal* as "Leaner and Meaner than Unix"). Because it is a disk-based operating system, OS9 is in theory as vulnerable as MS-DOS or any other disk-based operating system to viruses.

"In practice, though, to date I know of not one authenticated report of a CoCo OS9 virus *ever* being discovered. This may in part be due to the fact that OS9 users are a serious lot, and a very tiny minority among computer users—especially 6809/CoCo OS9—and so tend to support each other and are by nature less likely to spend their time concocting diabolical nasties. That may sound a bit corny but actually probably *is* to some real degree true.

"In the Portable Place, the Tandy 100 and 200 are relatively immune to any virus, again by virtue of the fact that their operating software is in the form of ROM-based firmware, so in the worst case, a freezing cold start will wipe out any viral infection.

"In the case of the MS-DOS–based lap portables, the issues are of course the same as those with MS-DOS desktop machines.

"Although real viruses have been created for MS-DOS machines, these are extremely rare, and roughly 99.99 percent of the time someone thinks a problem is due to a virus; it is instead due to software misuse, damaged software, or a hardware failure of some kind (the latter being relatively unlikely, too). Thus, at present, I for one am not honestly very worried about viruses, and (please take no offense here) tend to watch all the hysteria about them with just a little amusement.

"Since viruses can be created to merge with and contaminate the operating system in any of a number of ways, there does not seem to me any means of a sysop protecting users against viruses in any practical sort of way, apart from employing top notch assembly language programmers with extreme familiarity with MS-DOS operating system at the machine level to disassemble totally and analyze every program posted. This, of course, is a logistical and financial impossibility.

"Beyond that, it is hard for me to imagine any other means of dealing with the 'viral threat' than carefully examining any member report of problems that might be associated with a file one has downloaded. Of course, as we all note, software here is 'as is' and 'at your own risk.'"

Michael A. Banks, science fiction and computer book author, and manager of Science Fiction Group has found what he feels to be the ideal solution.

"We are concerned with the virus problem. After all, science fiction writers have long predicted it. But I let my Assistant Manager handle the actual checking out. He seems to know something about the subject."

(The author of this book in addition to managing the Writers Group is also assistant manager in the SF Group.).

One Man's Opinion

Now, I get to talk for me! As manager of Delphi's Writers Group for the past two years, the threat of viruses, Trojans, and logic-bombs has been a fact of life. There are over 300 programs now in the Writer's Software topic of my database. And, while system-wide and group disclaimers protect us from a legal standpoint, users certainly won't come back if they get a bad program.

I started using the *CHK4BOMB* program from the first. It's pretty simple (and was designed more for Trojans than viruses, having come out in 1985). You enter "CHK4BOMB <filename>" for a listing of all ASCII strings, and potentially dangerous disk activity. You get warning messages such as "****WARNING**** This program writes to absolute sectors. The possibility exists to overwrite important data." Or

"****WARNING**** This program FORMATS a disk! All data on the disk could be lost!"

A brave soul (or at least dedicated), I also run programs on my system before making them public in the Writers Group on Delphi. As might be expected, I've been burned. The FAT on my hard disk was trashed by a program that purported to be a "directory packer." After that, I also started using WPHD.COM, a nifty little utility that "write protects" your hard disk.

Now, of course, things are much better. Because of writing this book, I am receiving all sorts of virus protection and detection programs for review. I've taken to trying out all programs submitted or that I intend to upload to the Writers Group with a variety of these programs.

The recent programs in Writer's Software are probably the most thoroughly checked programs on any of the networks (grin). This does not mean a virus-infected program will never slip in, just that it's much more difficult now than it used to be.

Mike Riemer: Providing a Firm Foundation

FoundationWare's Mike Riemer is enthusiastic about his company's products (both the products and Mike himself have good reputations in the field). FoundationWare takes a somewhat different approach to fighting viruses.

"We do FAT table backup like *PC Tools* and *Mace*," Mike said, describing FoundationWare's programs. "We do FAT table recovery, we do low-level partition check and recovery—battery cellular recovery for AT&T. In that vein, we compete with people like Norton and Mace and we do it all automatically.

"We also provide what's called user control, which is a 600-byte memory resident program that prevents anything getting into memory that hasn't been approved to get there. So, with that a system manager can control what software is being run on a system.

"In addition to all that, we do a direct disk I/O monitor to make sure a bomb doesn't go off or someone doesn't accidentally format the hard disk. Generally, most of our competitors do one or two of those things. We have eight modules now, all in the same package. They are optional and have different switches to turn them on or off, and can be regulated for specific security levels.

"Generally, people like to hear the philosophy behind a product. Ours is if you are going to deal with the consumer, especially MIS people (Manager Information Systems) you have to provide them with tools which are useful in their environment. Give them control.

"The major problem inside of corporations, excluding the end user for a second, is the fact that people just bring in software that they are not supposed to. With our program, they can't do that. Nothing but nothing that hasn't been approved will run.

"A funny thing. Hal Highland came up to us at an Expo. He had six or eight viruses in his briefcase. He kept sticking in one after another and trying to run it. Obviously none of them were approved to run and wouldn't. We got a pretty good chuckle out of it.

"We're coming out with what we call 'blue disk' technology. We have the ability with our user interface to create external databases, so we made signature checks of a couple of the largest public domain and shareware libraries in the world and put them on a disk. So if you download a program, you can check it against your Blue Disk, which is a floppy disk, and see whether that version you just downloaded is one of the ones approved as being virus-free."

Mike Riemer and FoundationWare may be contacted at 2135 Renrock Rd., Cleveland, OH 44118, phone 1-800-722-8737.

More Experts than Room

There are several other people whose comments we wanted to add to this chapter, but lack of space prevents it. Ron Benvenisti at Worldwide Data was especially helpful, as was Dennis Director at Director Technologies, Larry DiMartin of Computer Integrity Corporation, Pam Kane and her fabulous *Dr. Panda,* and many others.

One of few really reassuring things about the computer virus problem is the high caliber of the people *fighting* viral infection. How can the sickies prevail when all the good guys and gals are on the side of right and might?

6
CORPORATE INITIATIVES FOR PC DATA SECURITY

Pamela Kane
President Panda Systems

The strength of a chain is its weakest link.

Old Proverb

Pam Kane's Panda Systems has been featured on the front page of The Wall Street Journal *(June 17,1988) and included in several of the major computer magazines. Dr. Panda utilities are one of the most highly rated virus-fighting systems currently available. "His round, soft and furry exterior," writes Hal Nieburg about* Dr. Panda *in the June* Computer Shopper *(page 316), "is deceiving. Inside is a set of three utilities that contain the heart of a tiger, the unrelenting persistence of an Inspector Hercule Poirot, and the savvy and skill of a James Bond . . ." Panda Systems also develops custom installation programs and additional security and data protection utilities for sensitive operations.*

Destructive code, whether virus, worm, Trojan Horse or a combination, seems to have proliferated in a constant and direct ratio to the number of personal computers in use. IBM's original estimate of PC sales was less than one-half million; no one could envision in 1980 that the personal computer would become a standard tool of corporate America in a few short years.

Had the architects of the PC been able to see the future, the operating system might have included many of the security safeguards standard on the larger computers targeted for corporate use. On the other hand, if the PC operating system had been more sophisticated and arcane, PC acceptance and growth could have been sharply limited by the increased difficulty of use.

An Achilles Heel

The best example of DOS's elementary nature is the FORMAT command. Any user able to type FORMAT can render an entire disk's data unusable, at least temporarily. Fortunes have been made by utility software vendors who provide "fixes" for the "holes" in DOS. Countless corporate overhead hours have been expended in developing end-user interfaces that minimize the possibility of inadvertent data destruction. It is the very simplicity of the PC's operating system that creates the environment where viruses can grow.

Just as the simplicity of DOS allows the easy incursion of destructive code, it provides for simple and inexpensive methods to prevent data destruction. Further, executable programs for personal computers, whether commercial or proprietary, may be replaced rapidly, allowing security techniques to focus on data and work product.

Practically and pragmatically, viruses are a fact of life in the late 1980s; they will continue to be spread, innocently for the most part, and responsible users and managers will take positive steps to prevent data loss from destructive code just as from any other source.

Experience tells us that the possibility of data loss due to destructive programs can reasonably be compared to the possibility of data loss due to power reductions or failures. Just as a surge protector is an essential part of a PC's hardware configuration, data protection procedures and utilities should be an essential part of system software configurations.

Looking back to the early days of the IBM PC-AT, another example is worth pointing out: Careful users and managers planned for *when* the drive would crash and spent no time at all on *if*.

Areas of Concern in Corporate Security

The three areas corporate security managers must consider in developing policies and procedures and the selection of data protection software are *Risk Assessment and Management, Cost/Benefit Analyses,* and *Human Resources.*

Risk assessment can involve lengthy and convoluted studies, particularly difficult when data loss or destruction for any reason is a taboo subject for publication in the corporate world. Using the example above, managers who choose not to include surge protectors in their installations are consciously taking an identifiable risk; failing to use antivirus procedures and software constitutes at least an equal risk.

Cost/Benefit Analysis is more straightforward. The cost of returning a single PC to service following data destruction can be calculated by adding technical support time, loss of productivity, and the cost of data recovery or re-creation. The cost of security software programs may be calculated in a similar fashion: the cost of the software program itself with costs of installation, training, and user support added.

Human Resources concerns are the most subtle and the most important. People costs far outweigh the costs of hardware or software in any organization. Training may be ineffective or confusing. Additional decision-making responsibility, particularly if the consequences of an error are great, is often unwelcome and stress-producing. Changes to the operation of a familiar system inevitably result in loss of productivity, if only for a brief time.

The ideal antiviral security procedures and software, therefore, will be absolutely unseen to the user *unless* there is evidence of potential data destruction at the end user level. While the end users should be relatively uninvolved in data security on the software level, managers and power users must be provided with powerful tools to prevent data destruction and to recover lost work product.

The ratio of end users to managers and technical support staff must also be considered in the development of security solutions and the associated budgeting. PC support departments are frequently understaffed and underbudgeted. Many companies rely on outside contractors for many services, often with a resulting lack of control or direction. These factors must also be given serious consideration in the planning process.

Difficulty may be encountered by PC managers or security administrators in "selling" the cost of such programs to the department heads who will ultimately "pay the bill." It is a Catch-22 of corporate reality that, should disaster strike, these same department heads will take the PC staff to task for failing to provide adequate security.

Prevention Techniques

Common sense, DOS functions, and standard commercial utilities will enable managers to begin a security program for safe computing and to perform some of the basic functions of anti-virus utilities. The following activities and functions can be extremely effective:

1. Add the CHKDSK command to AUTOEXEC.BAT. If the number of hidden files or disk space available changes, find the reason before using the system.
2. Prepare a "clean model" disk containing at least COMMAND.COM, IBM/MS DOS, IBMBIO/MSIO. Add other target files a virus writer might predict to be on a disk such as CONFIG.SYS, AUTOEXEC.BAT or 123.EXE. Write-protect the disk. Write a batch file using the DOS COMP command to check the selected files for changes or include the COMP function in AUTOEXEC.BAT. If a file has been changed, assume it's corrupted. Replace the file with a clean version. *Do not* assume the virus has disappeared.
3. Write batch files for COPY and FORMAT functions that include a CHKDSK on the target disk after the DOS operation. A system disk with a label will show three hidden

files, DOS, BIO/IO and the label. If additional hidden files are present, a virus may have been passed. **Note:** some copy-protected programs install hidden files.

4. Change the attributes of system or predictable files to Read Only using the DOS ATTRIB command or a utility.
5. Maintain an up to date hardcopy of your directories and their contents. TREE>lPT1 prints the directory structure. DIR>lPT1 for each subdirectory prints complete information about a directory's contents. Watch for unexplainable changes in file size or addition of new files.
6. Use only software from reliable sources. If using public domain/shareware/freeware, contact the writer/distributor to compare file date and file size before using. If the share/freeware does not include a contact address or telephone number, *do not use it.* Say no to "borrowware."
7. Begin the habit of clean boot operating system use before detection activities. Prepare a clean boot ["CB"] disk by turning off the PC, inserting an original DOS disk in A: and turning the power on. Type DISKCOPY A: A: and follow screen prompts. Use the write-protected duplicate as a clean boot disk.
8. Before copying data from a floppy to hard drive, cold boot and use CHKDSK to look for any hidden files. If hidden files other than the DOS LABEL 0-byte file are present, *do not* copy the data.
9. Always reFORMAT used floppies. A format from C: followed by cold boot and CHKDSK may detect a virus but produce a bad disk. For a cleaner result, format all disks after a cold boot.
10. Always download data to a floppy disk and look for hidden files on the floppy with CHKDSK. Run communications and .ARC programs from floppies after a cold boot.
11. Use a utility program to sort each subdirectory by date and time. Any date before 01/01/80 is a certain warning. Dates in the future should be carefully checked. Look for 00 in dates and times and any time greater than 23:59:59.
12. Sort on file size. Be alert for unusually large or 0-byte files. Compare file sizes with your hardcopy. Any change in .COM, .EXE, .BAT, or .SYS files should raise a warning flag.

13. Sort on file name. If a program is called by .EXE (123 for example) and a file with the same name and the extension .COM is present, this spells serious trouble. The .COM file executes first in the DOS hierarchy. Look for filenames that seem odd according to your naming conventions.
14. Another sort, this time on extension. You might not pick up DBASE.EVL or a file in the 123 subdirectory with .WK8 as an extension the first time through.
15. Remove suspicious files with a utility to WIPE them. Do not use the DOS DEL function that merely replaces the first letter of the filename so it won't show on a DIR. The file remains in place until written over.
16. Evaluate the risk factor for an individual system or installation. Any access of external data from disk, network, or modem entails risk.
17. Develop procedures and utilities that oversee or limit transfer of data among PCs. Network with other users for ideas and solutions.
18. Understand the meaning and operation of virus, worm, and Trojan Horse programs. The seeding of a virus from one system to another is a separate event from the operation of any destructive code the virus may implant. Worms wait for a signal such as a specific date or "x" numbers of access of "Y.EXE" to execute. Trojan Horse programs execute with the first access.

The above procedures, though based in sound practice, are time and effort intensive and, therefore, appropriate only for managers and the small group of experienced PC professionals in any organizational group. The large time requirement and the low security level achieved must be balanced against commercial utility products.

Virus Detection and Protection Software

According to the trade press, there are more than 100 antiviral software packages available, ranging in price from $10 shareware to thousands of dollars when a CD-ROM approach is used. Evaluation of the various products and approaches can be costly and time-consuming once an initiative is identified.

Virus detection programs or those that "inoculate" against particular "strains" of virus should be eliminated out of hand. It's impossible to conceive of a software program that can constantly be refreshed to counter the destructive code that just appeared yesterday. The cost involved in an almost constant update/upgrade situation is unacceptable for even the smallest installations.

Programs that require significant training or decision-making at end user levels are also to be avoided. A $20 package that requires $200 per user in training is not a bargain.

The ideal antivirus software for corporate use should be absolutely transparent to the user until potentially destructive activity is identified.

If this sounds too easy, consider again the simplicity of PC/MS-DOS coupled with the goal of a virus—to place itself in as many places as possible as often as possible. There are only three required and therefore, absolutely predictable files on a PC. These are COMMAND.COM, DOS, and BIO/IO. Next in predictability are files with extensions .COM, .EXE, and .SYS. Antiviral software that constantly checks for changes to such files and looks for changes in the hidden file structure will identify most virus incursions, even before they can begin their dirty work.

Should the presence of a virus not be identified, there are only four likely destructive activities, thanks again to the elementary nature of DOS. The four are: destruction of the boot sector, scrambling the initial bytes of the file allocation table, a logical format of any drive, or a virtual format of the default hard drive. By eliminating the possibility of any of these four events, antiviral software can provide an almost perfect foil for destructive programming.

By logical extension, the presence of destructive code is identified at the same time that data loss is prevented.

The "Yeah, but what if..." contingent in any organization may be counted on to develop scenarios where such a basic software approach will be defeated or circumvented. Clearly, no software will be 100 percent foolproof, especially against intentional sabotage. *The overriding goal must be to provide the highest security level at the lowest cost with the least intrusion.*

The port of entry for PC viruses should also be given careful consideration. Most destructive code is unwittingly brought into the workplace by computer literate employees. Employees who use home computers for both work and hobbies and employees seeking additional education in the computer field are the significant carriers. It would be unwise, to say nothing of unenforceable, to attempt to limit the external use of PCs by valuable employees.

Other Protective and Recovery Measures

Many companies are also attempting to ban the use of public domain and/or shareware programs on corporate machines. This is also policy that is practically unenforceable. Every PC guru, whether a member of the technical support staff or a departmental local expert has his or her own tool kit of favorite utilities.

Many of the best utilities available and in use today are in the public domain and are freely shared among users. Power users are, at least by reputation, highly independent sorts and often have strong opinions on methodology. This, combined with the tradition of sharing information among PC users would render such policies useless in practice. It's far better to institute "clean room" procedures for public domain programs. The increased employee involvement not only provides a significant benefit, but also a level of protection for possible licensing or copyright problems that might accrue to the company.

The business that is truly committed to human relation concerns will also provide home PC users with antiviral software and utilities, thereby further involving the employee with the chosen positive solution.

A written protocol should be developed for use by the technical support staff in case of a suspected virus attack. Such a document should include strong cautions not to construe any anomaly of operation as a virus situation without careful evaluation. It should also resist the temptation to reformat a hard drive immediately.

The best procedure is to simply swap out either the CPU or hard drive of the PC in question so troubleshooting and evaluation can take place without a serious loss of productivity.

If data backups are not available, data should be unloaded from the suspect PC using the DOS COPY command following a clean boot. Ideally, the replacement drive should be formatted and all standard applications software installed. If additional programs are required, they should be loaded from original disks, *not* copied from the questionable system.

If a working virus is identified, immediate and stringent quarantine measures should be implemented as well as mounting a search for any and all disks that were in contact with the virus site. It's difficult to state any general rules for these measures as the "patient zero" PC could be a stand-alone workstation with negligible access to other machines or it could be a node on a 500-PC local area network. If the virus leaves an identifiable footprint such as a message hidden within COMMAND.COM or a hidden file, any hard drive or disk exposed to the infected PC should be examined.

Commercial utilities that search for text strings ("@#$& YOU!") are readily available. Simple programs can also be written in assembly language and DOS DEBUG can be used to examine files.

Conclusions

The search for virus code can be lengthy and exhausting; recovery of lost data may be impossible. Data files on infected machines should be transferred with the utmost care and carefully inspected for accuracy. Infected disks should be physically destroyed and infected hard drives reformatted using FDISK from a clean boot. (The virtual, rather than logical, format of a hard drive is essential to remove all traces of virus code.)

Above all, don't trust to luck. Install viral-protection software and institute the procedures recommended above. Being safe is infinitely better than being sorry. If troubles persist, call a professional in the field of virus removal.

7
THE CASE OF THE GERBIL VIRUS THAT WASN'T

Raymond M. Glath
President, RG Software Systems, Inc.

Imagination rules the world.

Napoleon I (1769–1821)

RG Software Systems is the manufacturer of the Disk
Watcher *"disaster prevention" utility, and* PC Tracker,
*used by many large corporations to keep track of their per-
sonal computers. Ray Glath, its president, is a very
knowledgable virus fighter. We feel the amusing incident
he relates below is exceptionally appropriate for this book.*

It was a quiet, pleasant Friday afternoon when we received the
urgent call from the pastor of a small Pennsylvania church.
Quite upset, he expressed his need to immediately purchase our
antivirus product as he had lost a major section of his doctoral
thesis, along with many other files, to the "Gerbil" virus.

"All of a sudden, the word GERBIL appeared in the upper
left corner of my screen; footprints were scattered all over the
display and my system locked up" he exclaimed. "When I
turned the system off and on again, my document was gone ...
All that work lost." Upon questioning, the pastor stated that he

had used nothing but legitimate, purchased, professional software other than a DOS update disk he had received from his dealer.

Appalled at the thought of an innocent man of the cloth being attacked by an anonymous virus writer, we requested that he send us a copy of the disk he was using so we could attempt to track down this dastardly culprit.

After many hours of painstaking analysis, we determined that his disk simply contained a normal DOS system, several programs, and nothing unusual. Further discussions with the good pastor led to the discovery that this problem only appeared when he was using a specific commercial word processor, and he had returned the package to the store where he bought it. "With your antivirus package installed, I've had no further problems," he said.

Something just didn't sound right. We decided to purchase a copy of the package in question, and when we looked through the program code, lo and behold, there it was...: "GERBIL.DOC", "GERBIL.2" and several other uses of the word GERBIL... right there in the middle of this commercial package's program code!

We immediately contacted the publisher of the word processing system to alert them to the fact that we found something suspicious in their package and were continuing to research the matter. They responded that they had no reports of problems of this nature and that the package had been on the market for six months in many installations.

They did recognize the term GERBIL however, because that was the project Code Name while it was in development.

Aha... a clue.

As it turns out, the GERBIL references were never removed from the production version of the system. Each word processing document begins with an internally used id record that starts off with—you guessed it—GERBIL.DOC.

Additionally, this package allows you to bring program and other supporting files into the word processor as you would any other document.

And guess what some of the files begin with? Right again—GERBIL.

The Footprints?

Well, they turned out to be the happy faces, spade, club diamond, and other symbols you'll see when program code consisting of low value ASCII characters appears on a display. (They sure looked like footprints to the pastor. He didn't know what else to call them.)

In the meantime, fearful that he had been thoroughly infected by a virus and wanting to be sure that it would go no further, the pastor used his disk recovery utility to locate all occurrences of the word GERBIL on his disk, and he proceeded to erase all sectors that had the word GERBIL appearing. Now *all* his documents are unreadable; *all* his work is lost.

Did he ever contact the word processing publisher for support on the problem? Yes. No one had any idea what he was talking about. He also contacted his computer dealer, the regional rep for the computer system he was using, and the store where he bought the word processing package. His efforts were all to no avail.

Are there any lessons to be learned from this sad tale? You betcha!

Lessons for Software Publishers

Especially now that the concerns regarding viruses are high, let's start using less cute code names for projects. And when the project is complete and ready for commercial distribution, let's remove all references to the code name.

For those products already on the market with cute or questionable terminology embedded, let the customer support personnel in on it so the end users can have their fears allayed without causing major heartache.

Lessons for End Users

Every unusual event does not a virus indicate.

Make sure you have a static free environment surrounding your computer.

Immediately after encountering a strange event, make notes in as detailed a form as possible, regarding each step you performed in the few moments preceding the event. You'll need these to help the manufacturer's customer support person-nel determine corrective actions for you. And you may have to repeat them several times. You should be prepared to answer questions such as these:

What job were you running?
Precisely what were you doing?
What keys did you press?
Did the power fail?
Did the plug get pulled?
What file were you working on?
Have you had any recent hardware problems while
running any job?

Run the DOS CHKDSK program on the disk you were using. If the disk has been partially damaged by a power surge/drop/outage or static charge, you can encounter very strange results. If CHKDSK reports errors on a given disk, you'll need to check all the files from that disk to see if they're still intact.

Check with the tech support group from the publisher of the product you were using. In addition to the above details, you should also be prepared to give them the names of any TSR software you were using at the time, a description of your hardware configuration, and your DOS version number.

Finally, if you're concerned about your susceptibility to acquiring a virus, it may be helpful to install an antivirus pro-gram that could alert you to a possible virus problem.

But, you've got to exercise care in the selection of such a program. One that's been thrown together quickly without re-gard to compatibility and false alarm issues can be more troublesome than an actual virus.

8
IBM PCs AND COMPATIBLES

When most the world applauds you, most beware; 'tis often less a blessing *than a* snare.

Rev. Edward Young (1683–1765)

If those twisted and despicable few who concoct viruses have a favorite song, it is surely "Send in the Clones!"

The standard that IBM set back in 1981 with the personal computer has resulted in *millions* of computers that all can run the same software. Inexpensive compatibles or clones of the IBM PC can be ordered from any of the myriad of computer magazines for prices in the $500 range.

Thousands upon thousands upon *thousands* of public domain and shareware programs are available. The base of commercial programs is in the many tens of thousands. Businesses, schools, and individuals buy IBM or compatible computers because of these huge software resources.

Overall—with apologies to the Mac people for pointing out what is, alas, true—the most important work is done on IBM and compatible machines. The reason is simple (and one which Apple keeps trying unsuccessfully to overcome): There are so many more business-oriented programs available for IBM personal computers and clones that a large corporation doesn't hesitate as to which personal computer to buy in quantities.

As Ross Greenberg pointed out in Chapter 5, a corporation the size of General Electric, for example, might have a network of 40,000 PCs or more. This same propensity for choosing IBM compatibles applies to the majority of companies, institutions, and individuals who do *serious* work on a personal computer.

Craig Zarley, Feature Editor for *PC Week* wrote (April 26, 1988 issue, page 41): "PCs are the biggest capital asset at many companies."

John Markoff, writing in *The New York Times'* "Business Day" (March 18, 1988, page 1) says ". . . Companies will have to monitor the software on personal computers used in the workplace."

Those of us who make a living with our computers have a big enough problem—our data integrity is exceptionally important. Companies, corporations, universities, and all the rest who use *networks* of personal computers have a problem that's directly proportional to the number of machines they have linked together. Each and every machine is a potential source of infection for the whole network!

Those who might only use their PC for fun must also worry about viruses and the *liability* you incur. If you pass along a virus to someone else, even though it was inadvertent, you may wind up in court. In fact, one of the first cases of this type was filed with the United States District Court, District of New Mexico on August 12, 1988 at 10:34 a.m. The plaintiff is a computer bulletin board operator who contends that a Trojan horse program named BBSMON.COM was uploaded to his board by the individual who the suit is against.

The lawsuit was authorized against the defendant "pursuant to 18 U.S.C. sec. 2707 and providing for injunctive relief against unlawful access to stored electronic communications."

For interested attorneys, jurisdiction was invoked "pursuant to 28 U.S.C., sec. 1331, 28 U.S.C., sec. 2001, 28 U.S.C., sec. 2202. This action is instituted pursuant to 18 U.S.C., sec. 2707." The initials U.S.C. stand for United States Code, the body of Federal laws.

In other words, IBM personal computers and the hundreds of compatible brands present an exceptionally large, slow-moving target. Concocters of viruses simply can't miss. Whether you're an individual end user or involved with a larger network of personal computers, the virus-makers have painted a big bull's-eye on your back. It's not fair, but IBM and clones comprise the major virus battleground right now.

The millions of PCs already in use are like a great fertile plain to computer viruses—much like Fertile Crescent that gave rise to the world's first great civilizations: the Sumerians, Ur, Babylonian, the Caldeans, the Medes, and Persians. Like they learned the hard way, it's time to start putting walls around the villages.

This does not mean to lock everyone out. In ancient days, doing so would have stifled trade. In today's Information Age, not being able to telecommunicate is stagnation and a foolish self-immobilization. So, like the Sumerians put gates in their village walls—letting the villages grow to cities through trade—we need to do the same thing.

In blunt words, if you have an IBM or compatible personal computer, you *need* virus protection and detection. Not having this opens yourself to losing valuable data and to being legally liable for unwittingly spreading viruses to others.

The remainder of this chapter gives a brief overview of a number of commercial, public domain, and shareware programs. This information will help you determine what programs are available and choose the best type of protection and detection for your IBM or compatible.

Note: Shareware and public domain products are available from the computer networks such as Delphi and CompuServe, and from many local boards. To insure you get an uncontaminated product (infected virus detection software is obviously less than reliable), it's best to download the program from a computer network where you can be sure the program has been checked, or from the program author's personal board. For example, Ross Greenberg maintains a BBS in his office on which the latest *clean* version of *Flu_Shot+* is available. So does Chuck Gilmore, author of *Ficheck*.

Shareware, by the way, means you can obtain and try the program, and register it only if *you* decide it's of benefit on your system. This is an honor system—if you don't register, you are expected to stop using the product.

Bombsqad

Product   BOMBSQAD.COM 1.3 (*Bomb Squad*)
          CHK4BOMB (*Check for Bomb*)
Company   Andy Hopkins
          26 Walnut Lane
          Swarthmore, PA 19081
Type   Freeware
          Available in IBMSW on CompuServe

These two programs have been around for several years, coming about originally to fight Trojans, bombs, and worms. They are almost classics, and the price is certainly right.

Bomb Squad (BOMBSQAD.COM), says Andy Hopkins, is *not* a game. It's a further attempt to prevent pranksters from destroying your data. The proliferation of the Trojan Horse type programs that purport to be games (but actually plant bombs in your system that format your hard disk or erase the disk directory) has prompted the writing of this program as well as CHK4BOMB.EXE, *Check for Bomb.*

CHK4BOMB.EXE reads the program file from disk and attempts to spot dangerous code and suspicious messages, but since code is often a function of runtime memory situations, it could miss spotting the bombs. BOMBSQAD.COM is a program that intercepts calls to the BIOS code in ROM as a suspicious program is run, displays what is going to happen during the call, and asks if you want to continue. You can abort or continue as you see fit.

"In the spirit of cooperation with fellow PC users and hoping to discourage those whose idea of a joke is destroying other people's valuable data," writes Andy, "I encourage you to make copies of this program and documentation and give it to anyone who may be susceptible to these pranksters. Users who frequently download BBS programs of unknown origin may find BOMBSQAD particularly useful. Complete rights to the program itself, and the routines used in the program, however, remain with the author, Andy Hopkins, through Swarthmore Software Systems."

C-4

Product *C-4 Antiviral Shield*
Company InterPath
4423 Cheeney Street
Santa Clara, CA 95054
(408) 988-3832
Type Commercial
$39.95

Its manufacturer describes *C-4* as running permanently in the background of your system. It monitors all system activity, including program loads, BIOS calls, interrupt requests and accesses to system and application files. The monitor checks for characteristic viral replication activity—such as attempts to write to executable programs or DOS system files; access to a disk's boot sector; attempted modification of COMMAND.COM and other techniques that viruses typically use to reproduce themselves. *C-4* also checks for activities that indicate a virus is active and attempting to destroy or corrupt the system. These activities include access to the system's file allocation table, low-level formats, and other low-level disk access requests.

If a virus does enter your system, *C-4* will identify the virus and prevent it from infecting any existing programs on your disks. It will freeze the virus and display a warning window, identifying the name of the offending program and the name of the file or disk area where it was attempting to replicate itself. Likewise, if your system was infected prior to installing *C-4* and an existing virus attempts to activate, it will be frozen before it can cause harm, and you will be notified.

Steve Gibson, writing in his "Tech Talk" column in *InfoWorld* (May 9, 1988) calls *C-4* one of "The two most effective virus detection monitors available . . ." (For the other one, see the description of *Flu_Shot+* below).

Caware

Product   *Caware*
Company   Chuck Gilmore
          Gilmore Systems
          P.O. Box 3831
          Beverly Hills, CA 90212-0831
          Voice: (213) 275-8006 BBS: (213) 276-5263
Type   Shareware
          $10 registration fee

Gilmore Systems offers a way in which you can allow your compiled *Turbo C* programs to check themselves for changes in their CRC or file size, thus detecting if a virus has modified them. Viruses have become a problem—altering *.EXE and *.COM files these days. Not just viruses, but hackers also modify shareware programs because they don't like looking at the opening screens.

If you're a programmer using *Turbo C,* you now have a means of protection. You can make your programs aware of their own CRC and file size—the two most likely things to change in the event of a virus or hacker attack. CAWARE.ARC, the archived file in which this system is distributed (available in CompuServe IBMSW and elsewhere) contains a READ.ME file, MAKAWARE.EXE (EXE initializer), EXAMPLE.C (sample source for using the checker), and six OBJs—one for each memory model you can link with your programs to offer you (or your program) security. This code offers protection that no external programs can offer.

"At least now," said Chuck Gilmore, "nobody can accuse *your* program of containing a virus. Although nothing's perfect, I'm sure some hacker will come up with a way of defeating this code manually, but it would be extremely difficult for a virus to alter or defeat this code."

As with all shareware, try it first. If you like it, send Gilmore Systems $10. In return for your $10, they will send you the source code. You'll receive:

EXEAWARE.C—source code needed to reproduce the EXEAWAR?.OBJ files.

MAKAWARE.C—source code needed to reproduce the MAKAWARE.EXE file.

If you register for $15 instead of $10, you get six months of full access to Gilmore's "Virus Info" BBS in addition to the source code (see the review of FICHECK for more information on the BBS; it's worthwhile). The "Virus Info" BBS deals strictly with the topic of computer viruses. You can download text, source, and programs all pertaining to computer virus prevention and detection. This is a great way to keep informed of the latest viruses going around.

Checkup

Product   *Checkup*
Company   Richard B. Levin
           BBSoft
           9405 Bustleton Ave.
           P.O. Box 14546
           Philadelphia, PA 19115
           Lab: (215) 333-6922
           BBS: (215) 333-6923
           BBS: (215) 635-5226
Type   Shareware
           $5 registration fee

Checkup is one of several excellent shareware answers to viral protection. Author Richard B. Levin describes the software's operation as being able to detect viral infections by comparing a target file's size, its incremental checksum, and its total checksum to previously stored baseline values. The program breaks the target filespec down to a series of randomly sized blocks of data. These data blocks may vary from one byte to near total file size. If the size of the file being checked is less than the block size selected, *Checkup* revises the block size downward. *Checkup*'s dynamic block size allocation allows files as small as one byte to be accurately checked.

Checkup scans and compares every byte of the target filespec on a block-by-block basis. If the recorded file size, any of the block checksum comparisons, or the checksum totals don't match, *Checkup* alerts the user that the target file has been altered and possibly infected.

Checkup's incremental file checksum technique is preferable to simply adding the bytes in a file and comparing past and present checksum totals. Future viruses may be intelligent enough to calculate a host file's checksum total, pad their own code with dummy characters to maintain total checksum integrity, and then infect. Such viruses, says Levin, would defeat other checksum calculation programs, but not *Checkup*.

"We believe it is impossible for a virus to maintain an accurate intra-block checksum. This is especially true when the checked block size varies from one byte to near the total file size; the method for calculating the checksum is unknown, and the results are encrypted."

To survive *Checkup*'s scrutiny, a virus would need to know the block size, exact calculation entry point, checksum calculation algorithm, and the encryption key *Checkup* used on the target filespec at initialization. The encroaching virus would then have the difficult (if not impossible) task of padding its own code with dummy characters, since the adjustments would have to occur every few hundred bytes. If a super-virus were able to achieve this high degree of adaptability, it would still be unable to operate in an internally scrambled condition.

The latest version of *Checkup* is available for downloading on the BBSoft Support BBSs. Support is also available through the BBSoft Lab. Please leave a message on the answering machine if your call is not answered personally. Long distance calls will be returned after 6:00 p.m. EST, collect.

Condom

Product   *Condom* (FCBIN.PAS version 1.01—June 1, 1988)
Company Jim Murphy
               CompuServe ID 74030,2643
Type   Public Domain Freeware

Dr. C. Everett Koop, the Surgeon General of the United States addresses the problem of AIDS: "The only protection against the virus, short of total abstinence is the use of a condom."

Jim Murphy applies this same philosophy to his antiviral program, which he generously placed in the public domain. The program is distributed as a file named CONDOM.ARC, and is available in such places as Chuck Gilmore's Virus Info Palladium computer bulletin board (see the review of *Ficheck* for the telephone number). It includes the *Turbo Pascal* source code so you can see exactly what you're getting and recompile it if you want to be absolutely certain it's clean.

"I first became aware of the existence of the software virus in magazine articles," Jim says in his documentation, "and I wondered what I could do to protect my computer from their insidious attack. The prime target was usually reported to be COMMAND.COM, although just about any program could be its target.

"I reasoned that if I could compare COMMAND.COM against a known healthy copy, I could be sure that at least it had not been contaminated. I figured I would use FC.EXE (file compare) that came with MS-DOS, in my AUTOEXEC.BAT file to check COMMAND.COM each time I booted up, and if there was a difference, flag it so I could replace COMMAND.COM before any damage was done.

"Let me regress for a minute. The demented individuals who write these viruses want to make sure it gets spread around, so they design them to work a few days, or a few boot ups after the virus installs itself. It is done this way to insure that the virus will be spread by formatting other disks, or looking at a directory in another drive that contains the program the virus installs itself in (usually COMMAND.COM). This being the case, you can most likely catch it when you boot up the computer for the next session. If it did its dirty work immediately, I would call it a Trojan horse problem, and that requires different techniques, although you could use some of those protection methods along with the one I am describing to get close to 100 percent protection.

"I wanted the boot up to be automatic, stopping only if COMMAND.COM was changed. Using FC.EXE would not work as it doesn't send an errorlevel code after it terminates, so I decided to write my own File Compare utility that would output an errorlevel code. I wanted it to be fast, and it would not have to show every byte that was different, just tell me that the two files were not identical. I could use FC.EXE later to get a complete report of the differences.

"I called my program FCBIN.EXE (File Compare Binary); it is written in *Turbo Pascal* version 4.0 and it will compare any file, reporting all the general differences, such as Date and Length, and that the bytes did not compare. It also tells you at which byte the first difference occurred.

"I decided to check all my files in the root directory as well by creating a subdirectory called ZROOT in which were placed uncontaminated copies of all the files in the root directory. The file copies were renamed for additional safety; COMMAND.COM is called CMD.BAK; CONFIG.SYS is called CFG.BAK, and so on.

Cop

Product   *Cop* (Command Obfuscation Processor)
Company Jack A. Orman
                 Box 858
                 Southaven, MS 38671
Type   Shareware
                 $15 registration fee

This program is used to encode a .COM program to make the data or programming techniques indecipherable. It will make hacking or modification of the program that much more difficult. This is not, the author points out, a surefire, guaranteed safeguard system, but is merely to keep the average programmer from tinkering with your code.

"It is not foolproof," Jack Orman said, "and I'm sure that an expert programmer can break the system easily."

Note: Only use COP.COM on copies of your programs, not the originals!

To encode a .COM program, type in the following:

COP [d:]filename code-phrase <ENTER>

Cop will read the program and by using the code-phrase, write a modified version back to the disk. The modified version is encoded and makes disassembling of the code quite difficult. Note that *Cop* writes over the original version of the file that's being processed. The *Cop* modified program will still run from the DOS prompt and perform just as the original.

Cop is available on a number of bulletin boards and the national networks. The Writers Group on Delphi has *Cop* and several of Jack Orman's other excellent shareware programs available for downloading. There is no charge for this service other than normal Delphi connect time.

Data Physician

Product   *Data Physician* Software Protection System, including *VirAlert*
Company   Digital Dispatch, Inc.
           55 Lakeland Shores
           St. Paul, MN 55043
           (800) 221-8091
           (612) 436-1000 (in Minnesota)
Type   Commercial
           $199

Data Physician is a set of programs designed to help protect your PC-DOS or MS-DOS computer system from software viruses and logic bombs. The programs consist of the following:

Datamd. This is the main virus protection, detection, and removal program. It allows you to detect whether an unauthorized change has occurred in any file or system area on your disk, and also allows the removal of certain types of viruses.

Padlock. Along with *Disklock* provides an intelligent disk write-protect function. They intercept attempted writes to disk that a virus may use as it infects or attacks your system. They also provide protection against logic bombs that don't spread on their own, but can attack in much the same manner as a virus.

Novirus works with the data created by *Datamd* and runs virus detection in background mode while you perform other tasks on your system. This can be helpful if you have many files to watch over, or if you want continuous security monitoring.

Antigen. Allows virus protection to be installed directly on any executable program. Each time a protected program is run, it checks itself for tampering and is capable of removing certain types of viruses on its own. *Antigen* is useful when it's not practical to have *Datamd* or *Novirus* in operation, or where the protected program needs to be widely distributed and you want it to continue to be protected.

Viralert is a program (actually a device driver) that runs continually in the background to intercept changes to executable and operating system files (.EXE, .COM, and .SYS). *VirAlert* also watches for changes to the boot record, and any disk formatting attempts.

Data Physician is a powerful, well-thought-out system with a lot of tools. The documentation is above average.

Disk Defender

Product   *Disk Defender*™
Company Director Technologies, Inc.
906 University Place
Evanston, IL 60201
(312) 491-2334
Type   Commercial (hardware)
U.S. Patent #4,734,851
$240

"In the war on computer viruses, while everyone else is trying to perfect the bow and arrow, Director Technologies is manufacturing a tank! It's called *Disk Defender.*"

As we discussed early in this book, the MS-DOS system of file management is very vulnerable. Viruses succeed, in most cases, simply because hard disks and floppies are wide open to infiltration and destruction. The *Disk Defender* system of plug in card and external control box rectifies this design deficiency of all IBM and compatible computers.

Dennis Director, president of the company, points out that *Disk Defender* operates independently of any software, and cannot be circumvented by *any* software. It can be used with multiple operating systems on one disk, and will work regardless of networking configurations. Disconnect the control box and the zone protect is locked in for maximum data safety.

Disk Defender automatically write-protects all or part of any fixed Winchester disk having an ST-506/412 standard interface. It does not affect the use of the second hard disk on two drive systems, but allows reading at all times.

Activation is by an external control box, which can be placed anywhere up to five feet from the computer system. The operator activates protection by placing the switch on the face of the control box in the desired protection mode. Three status lights keep the operator advised on disk access, reading, and writing functions.

The external control box can easily be removed if it's preferred that the operator not have access to the protected portion of the disk. Without the control box in place, the unit is in the Zone protect mode at all times, and no one can get access to the protected portion of the disk.

"Software cures," Dennis Director said, speaking of the virus problem, "are not the answer. The destructive virus, itself, is a piece of software. Of course, software can be developed to neutralize a particular virus, but it will not stop other viruses. The creator of that virus has but to change one small part of the code for that virus to easily thwart the original software 'cure.'"

Hardware, he points out, affords 100 percent protection against all viruses because the PC needs a device that makes it impossible for write signals to reach the hard disk and corrupt its stored programs. *Disk Defender* is such a device, and lets you select all or a portion of the hard disk as a protected zone. The programs and data files to be protected are placed in this protected zone of the hard disk.

Mr. Director said that IBM had even bought several of his units to protect its own large software library. Director Technologies is also working on a similar device for the Apple Macintosh series of computers.

The company also publishes the *Computer Virology* newsletter, which is offered free. Contact the above address for more information.

Disk Watcher

Product *Disk Watcher*
Company Raymond M. Glath
RG Software Systems
2300 Computer Avenue
Willow Grove, PA 19090
(215) 659-5300
Type   Commercial
$99.95

Disk Watcher is more than just another viral protection program, it's also *disaster prevention* software.

First, of course, it provides multiple lines of defense against viruses. Here's how the system of programs included in the Disk Watcher package handles viral protection.

The first program automatically checks all active disk drives and the computer's RAM for the presence of certain hidden virus characteristics when the computer is started. This program can also be run on demand at any time to check the disk in a specific drive.

Disk Watcher, itself, is a TSR program that when installed, monitors ongoing disk activity throughout all processing with a series of proprietary algorithms that detect the behavior characteristics of a myriad of virus programs. Depsite this, the product uses minimal overhead in processing time and false alarm reports.

Disk Watcher has the unique ability to differentiate between legitimate I/O activity and the I/O activity of a virus program. When an action occurs indicative of a virus attempting to reproduce itself, alter another program, set itself up to be automatically run the next time the system is started, or attempting to preform a massively damaging act, *Disk Watcher* will pop up. You will then have several options, one of which is to immediately stop the computer before any damage can be done.

Whenever the "Stop the computer" option is selected, both the application program screen image and *Disk Watcher*'s screen image will be automatically set to the system printer before the machine is stopped. This helps in performing an effective analysis of the problem.

Disk Watcher also protects against certain other mishaps such as accidentally or carelessly losing valuable data, or just time and paper wasting actions such as unintentionally hitting Shift-PrtSc.

The program also protests against a full disk error message, accidental format of a hard disk, the printer not being ready, and the system date and time not being set (or the battery in the clock expiring). Numerous file and disk management tasks are also added, all for an expenditure of about 40K of RAM (the program is a TSR). *Disk Watcher* works on IBM PCs, ATs, PS/2s, and compatibles.

It is also a very well-behaved program, being able to co-exist with a variety of other TSRs without causing lockups (a condition not true of products tested from several other companies). *Disk Watcher* is a viral protection system (and more) that you should take a serious look at.

Dr. Panda

Product   *Dr. Panda Utilities*
Company Pam Kane
           Panda Systems
           801 Wilson Road
           Wilmington, DE 19803
           (302) 764-4722
Type   Commercial
           $79.95

Panda Systems and their virus-fighting software offer the viral detection and protection package described below. Their system is one of the highest rated for effectiveness.

The *Dr. Panda Utilities* detect virus, worm and Trojan horse programs. *Dr. Panda* is a three-part software approach that should be used in conjunction with sound management practices.

Physical, the virus detection utility, compares essential system files and user selected files against an unique installation record. The system status is reported onscreen each time *Physical* is run. If a file has been changed, the filename is displayed onscreen. Any change in a system file, *.SYS, *.COM, *.EXE, *.OVL or other program file may indicate a virus. *Physical* also reports the name and location of all hidden files on a disk at each operation.

Labtest displays the hidden ASCII strings of a selected file after reporting warning messages for calls bypassing DOS. Through the function key interface, the user may scroll through the file onscreen, perform basic editing functions, and direct output to a file or printer. Help screens assist in identifying and analyzing potentially destructive code.

Monitor automatically intercepts disk operation calls that request a format of any drive or writes to the File Allocation Table of C: (or the first designated hard drive). The user may also select additional disk operations for checking (Read, Write, Verify) at installation. Control of a program passes to the keyboard at each interrupt with a Proceed/Bypass option. *Monitor* is particularly effective against Trojan horse programs that destroy data immediately as part of their operation.

The utilities provide a basic security system for PC/MS-DOS microcomputers. Viruses in computers, as in their users, come from contact.

Panda Systems recommends the following: Any system that *ever* accesses external data is at risk. To practice safe computing, *never* use an unknown program without checking it first. Using the *Dr. Panda Utilities* from the original Dr. Panda disk will check a PC's files for any changes (destructive or benign) and allow evaluation of any file for potentially harmful operations. The responsibility for good computing practices depends upon computer users and managers. Panda Systems' consulting and technical staff are available to assist in troubleshooting advanced processes and development of security policies and procedures.

Ficheck

Product   *Ficheck* 4.0
Company Chuck Gilmore
           Gilmore Systems
           P.O. Box 3831
           Beverly Hills, CA 90212-0831
           Voice: (213) 275-8006 BBS: (213) 276-5263
Type   Shareware
           $15 registration fee

    Ficheck is one of several effective *shareware* virus protection programs. Don't let their low price scare you off; some of these programs are worth far more than the low registration fees. This one, for example, is but a mere $15. Below is a description of how *Ficheck* works, as explained in the documentation that comes with version 4.0.

    There are some viral-fighting programs available such as *Flu_Shot+,* and versions of *Vaccine.* These programs attempt to block viruses from doing things that viruses typically do. They attempt to block any altering of COMMAND.COM or your other operating system's system files. They try to alert you of low-level disk writing. These programs look for other things as well, but may slow your system down as a result. Some require you to make lists of approved programs and TSRs. The problem with these programs are that they're running on your system which may contain a virus that looks for these particular programs and renders them inactive or makes them think everything's okay while they do their dirty work.

    Ficheck is a program that differs from vaccine-type programs and other programs that attempt to find, block, or alert you to viruses. *Ficheck* does none of these things. As a matter of fact, *Ficheck* can't even be run from your fixed disk! *Ficheck* is a preventive medicine program that takes an "x-ray" of your entire fixed disk(s) and logs it to a file. *Ficheck* logs the date, time, size, attribute, and CRC (Cyclic Redundancy Check) of every file on your fixed disk(s). It looks for differences in all these things whenever you decide to run it again and alerts you to any changes. Any changes potentially mean a virus is at work. Viruses have to alter files in some way in order to spread themselves.

Ficheck should *not* be placed on your fixed disk—it will only run from a floppy, and furthermore, it won't even run from a floppy unless you boot DOS from a floppy.

Why all the hassle of booting from and running from a floppy? It's Simple.

If you boot from a fixed disk, you may boot from an infected copy of your operating system, start an infected TSR, have an infected device driver, or run an infected program. If you boot from floppy, you don't give the viruses on your fixed disk a chance to become active. Therefore, the first thing you should do to prepare for using the *Ficheck* program is:

1. Boot DOS from your original distribution disk.
2. Format a bootable floppy (not the distribution disk); use the command FORMAT A:/S
3. Copy FICHECK.EXE to the newly formatted disk.
4. Diskcopy this new disk for as many fixed disk drives or logical drives you have on your system and label each one for a specific drive.

Ficheck searches all file attributes. Once processing has started, Ficheck starts a timer and when processing finishes, *Ficheck* prints how long it ran. On computers running at 4.77 Mhz such as the original IBM XTs, *Ficheck* may take a while to complete its job. On computers such as the IBM PS/2 Model 80 running at 20 Mhz, *Ficheck* flies right through. Gilmore Systems has incorporated fast algorithms so *Ficheck* will run through your system as fast as possible.

*　　　　*　　　　*

In conjunction with the shareware and commercial products offered by Gilmore Systems, Chuck Gilmore also runs the VIP (Virus Info Palladium) computer bulletin board in Los Angeles (1-213 276-5263). You can call this board and download FICHECK4.ARC from the FREE area of the FILES menu. You can do this regardless of whether you're a registered user of the BBS or not.

If you become a registered user of *Ficheck,* Gilmore Systems will automatically mail you the latest commercial version of *Xficheck* on disk. *Xficheck* is a copyrighted commercial program (nonshareware, non–public domain) that's offered to their registered users at no charge. *Xficheck* is distributed exclusively from the Virus Info Palladium BBS—no distribution to the public by other BBS systems or by any other means is allowed without the prior written permission of Gilmore Systems.

If you've registered your *Ficheck* program with Gilmore Systems (remember, shareware authors have to eat, *too*), your access level will be upgraded within 72 hours of your first call. Until then, all you can really do is download anything in the [F]ree area of the [F]iles section. The other sections will not be available to you until your access level has been updated. Also note that the [M]essage section will not allow you to read or write messages (you can only scan) until upgrade has been implemented.

If you don't have a copy of FICHECK, you can download FICHECK4.ARC from the Free area of the Files section. Instructions in the documentation explain how to register. Also available in the Free area is a sample listing (SAMPLE.LST) of some of the antiviral and virus related text files, programs, source code, and other relevant files available to you for downloading once you've registered. You are allowed to download anything in the Free area—you don't need to be a registered user to download from that area.

Both *Ficheck* and the VIP BBS are worth checking out. Chuck Gilmore and his Gilmore Systems have become one of the respected names in the ongoing fight against computer viruses.

Flu—Shot+

Product   *Flu—Shot+* 1.4
Company Ross M. Greenberg
            Software Concepts Design
            594 Third Avenue
            New York, New York 10016
            BBS: (212)-889-6438 1200, 2400, N/8/1
Type   Shareware
            $10 registration fee

The original *Flu—Shot,* one of the first virus protection programs, now has a new name: *Flu—Shot+.* Some "worm" (as Ross Greenberg so aptly calls them) put out a program called FLUSHOT4 which was a Trojan. Greenberg opted to change the name.

"Besides," Greenberg said, "*Flu—Shot+* is the result of some real effort on my part, instead of being a part-time quick hack. I hope the effort shows."

Flu—Shot is now table driven. That table is in a file named FLUSHOT.DAT. It exists in the root directory on your C: drive. However, you can change its location to one of your choice so a worm can't create a Trojan to modify that file.

This data file allows you to write- and/or read-protect entire classes of programs. This means you can write-protect from damage all of your *.COM, *.EXE, *.BAT, and *.SYS files. You can read-protect all your *.BAT files so a nasty program can't even determine what name you used for *Flu—Shot+* when you invoked it.

Additionally, you can now automatically check programs when you first invoke *Flu—Shot+* to determine if they've changed since you last looked at them. Called checksumming, it allows you to know immediately if one of the protected programs has been changed when you're not looking. Additionally, this checksumming can even take place each time you load the program for execution.

Also, *Flu—Shot+* will advise you when any program "goes TSR." TSR stands for Terminate and Stay Resident, allowing pop-ups and other useful programs to be created. A worm could create a program that leaves a bit of slime behind. Programs like Borland's *SideKick,* a wonderful program and certainly not a Trojan or virus, is probably the best known TSR. *Flu_Shot+* will advise you if any program you haven't already registered in your FLUSHOT.DAT file attempts to go TSR.

Finally, *Flu_Shot+* will also now pop up a small window in the middle of your screen when it gets triggered. It also will more fully explain why it was triggered. The pop-up window means your screen won't get changed beyond recognition—unless you're in graphics mode when it pops up; this is a problem common to many TSR programs.

Steve Gibson, writing in his "Tech Talk" column in *InfoWorld* (May 9, 1988) calls *Flu_Shot+* one of "The two most effective virus detection monitors available..."

The right to use *Flu_Shot+*," Ross said, in explaining the shareware concept under which his viral-protection product is marketed, "is contingent upon your paying for the right to use it. I ask for ten dollars as a registration fee. This entitles you to get the next update shipped to you when available. And it allows you to pay me, in part, for my labor in creating the entire Flu_Shot series. I don't expect to get my normal consulting rate or to get a return equal to that of other programs which I've developed and sell through more traditional channels. That's not my intent, or I would have made *Flu_Shot+* a commercial program and you'd be paying lots more money for it.

"Some people are uncomfortable with the shareware concept, or believe there's no such thing as Trojan or Virus programs, and that a person who profits from the distribution of a program such as *Flu_Shot* must be in it for the money. I've created an alternative for these folks. I'll call it 'charityware.' You can also register *Flu_Shot+* by sending me a check for $10 made out to your favorite charity. Be sure to include a stamped and addressed envelope. I'll forward the money on to them and register you fully."

Guard Card

Product   Guard Card™
Company   NorthBank Corporation
          10811 NorthBank Road
          Richmond, VA 23333
          (804) 741-7591
Type   Commercial (hardware)
          $194

NorthBank takes a hardware approach to viral protection. Their *Guard Card* is a plug-in board that provides "true hardware-based write protection for your hard disk! It nails viruses and Trojans (and warts!) dead in their tracks."

The Guard Card prevents accidental erasures and formats when persons share a PC, such as in a networked system. It also protects turnkey user libraries from user error. The card supports one or two drives. One drive can be area-protected (Requires partitioning. Works with any ST-506 controller). A system reset button is included.

Ice

Product   ICE.COM (Intrusion Countermeasure Electronics
          COM File
          Security)
Company   Keith P. Graham
          c/o PC-Rockland BBS (914) 353-2157
Type   Freeware
          Available in IBMSW on CompuServe

Ice is a program that scrambles and compresses .COM files (not .EXE files) yet allows them to be fully functional. The program makes it difficult to alter the original program and it has the added bonus of compressing .COM files without detracting from their usefulness. Iced .COM files still run as they did before except they're usually smaller and disk load times are shorter. *Ice* offers protection against viruses in that *Ice* can scramble COMMAND.COM and make it difficult for viruses to attach themselves to the scramble program.

The format of the Ice command:

ICE FILE.COM encryption-key

FILE is the name of a .COM file to *Ice* and *encryption key* is a string of numbers and/or letters that will help make your scramble unique.

Ice will compress and scramble the .COM file and replace the original. It's important to have a backup of the original .COM file in case *Ice* doesn't work properly on a particular file.

"I have written," says Keith Graham, "an Ice Breaker for Iced programs and I am sure that any good hacker could also figure it out after awhile. No software resource can be protected entirely by software. I can only guarantee that *Ice* makes .COM files safer, not 100 percent safe."

Ice is distributed as freeware but remains the property of Keith P. Graham and is not for sale, but you are allowed to share it with your friends as long as no fee is associated with the copying of *Ice* or distribution of *Ice* other than nominal disk copy or access charges.

IFCRC

Product   *IFCRC*
Company   David Bennett
           Bennett Software Solutions
           151 West Geospace Drive
           Independence, MO 64056.
           CompuServe ID: 74635,1671
Type   Freeware
           Available in IBMSW on CompuServe

This program (compiled using Borland's *Turbo Pascal* 4.0 compiler) is for use in a batch file. It allows you to execute commands based on whether or not a certain file matches the given CRC value. The program can also be used to check the CRC value of a file (CRC stands for Cyclic Redundancy Check).

"Although I primarily wrote this program to execute a certain command based on whether a file has been altered or not," writes David, "it could also be used to check a daily transfer from a remote site or even used to check for computer viruses.

"I hereby release this program to the public domain (Guilt FreeWare!)."

Mace Vaccine

Product   *Mace Vaccine*
Company Paul Mace
               Paul Mace Software
               499 Williamson Way
               Ashland, OR 97520
               (503) 488-0224
Type   Commercial
               $20

Paul Mace is an extremely respected name in the field of IBM and compatible software. The *Mace Utilities* (version 4.1, $99.00) is one of the leaders in hard disk format recovery and maintenance. Their familiar ads featuring a Swiss Army knife appear in most major computer magazines. The *Mace Vaccine* antiviral package, just introduced as this book was being written, is currently being included free for purchasers of the *Mace Utilities.*

Mace Vaccine, says the company, is designed to warn you when unusual attempts are made to access vital disk areas and system files, not just by a computer flu or virus, but by any application that has no business modifying these vital areas of your disk. You can also raise the protection level to prevent any unauthorized access outside of DOS. This will stop any of the current viruses "before it stops you."

The unique feature that *Mace Vaccine* has over most other viral protection software is the option to increase or decrease levels of protection. Level 1 (the default) will write-protect the drive against access to vital areas and system files. Your permission is required before any vital area or file can be modified.

Level 2 provides all Level 1 protection of vital areas and files. Additionally, it write-protects the drive against all attempts at direct access. Only normal DOS applications are permitted to write, unless you grant permission.

Those things that aren't granted direct access include viruses, DOS format, CHKDSK/F and Debug, disk reorganizers such as *Mace UnFrag, Disk Optimizer, Norton SpeedDisk,* and disk sector editors such as Norton and *PC Tools.*

You may also turn *Mace Vaccine* off. This does not remove it from memory; it simply turns off protection. You can use this feature (judiciously) when there's a conflict with other software.

Mace Vaccine is a resident program, and takes up approximately 4,000 bytes (4K) of memory. It is most effective when placed first in your AUTOEXEC.BAT file. It's a solid effort from a solid company.

NōVirus

Product   *NōVirus*
Company Matt Hill
         MLH Software Systems
         1007 Chelten Parkway
         Cherry Hill, NJ 08034
         (609) 795-5257
Type   Shareware
         $10 registration fee

The earliest symptom of a virus, Matt Hill says in the documentation enclosed with *NōVirus,* is usually a change in the size of one or more of your system files. These are the files that most viruses will attack first.

The authors of viruses are concerned with one thing only—the destruction of data, and the more the better! For this reason, viruses are generally planted into the system files because they're the only files copied and run enough to do any substantial amount of damage. When a system disk becomes infected, the modifications to the system files will almost always be manifested in a change of the size or one or more of these files.

"Due to the fact that two out of these three files are invisible via the DIR command," Matt writes in explaining his logic philosophy of virus protection, "I have developed a utility called *NōVirus* which monitors the sizes of these files automatically."

When properly installed, *NōVirus* automatically monitors the sizes of system files on any system disk you choose. Every time it encounters a new disk, it will determine the sizes of each of the individual system files on that disk and store these figures onto the disk itself in a hidden, write-protected file. The next time you run *NōVirus* on that disk, it will find its file and compare the stored sizes to the current sizes of the files. If the sizes are the same, it's unlikely that the disk had become infected and *NōVirus* will quietly notify you of that fact. However, if *NōVirus* detects even the slightest change in the size of any of these files, it will give you adequate warning to that effect.

To initialize *NōVirus* on your hard disk drive, simply copy the program onto the disk. Matt suggests placing it into a utility or system subdirectory to which you have a path set up.

If you'd like to verify that your system files have actually been hooked or you are just curious to see what your system files are called, you may now obtain a formatted listing of all of the files that were identified as system files on your disk by entering:

C: \ >NOVIRUS /L

NōVirus will then perform a size-check and provide a listing of the system files as per your request. Please note that *NōVirus* does not detect the presence of a virus. It merely watches out for changes in the sizes of your system files after the time of the initial installation which may have been caused by viral modification. Although it's unlikely that your system is already infected, you may want to reinstall your operating system before using *NōVirus* for the first time.

To be effective, *NōVirus* needs to be run often. Matt suggests placing it into your AUTOEXEC.BAT. This should be enough, unless you do a reasonable amount of downloading or have reason to believe that your system may have come into contact with an infected disk. In this case, you may want to manually invoke the program at the DOS prompt immediately after you think a change may have taken place. You may accomplish this by typing:

C: \ >NOVIRUS

"A lot of time and hard work went into the planning and development of this product," writes Matt Hill, "and I'd like to think that my effort was not in vain. I have been using *NōVirus* for some time now and I feel that it's something that I can trust. I sincerely hope that you will feel the same way after you've gotten to know the program. It is my goal that if enough people take preventive measures like these we can stop the spread of the horrible computer virus."

SYSCHK1

Product   *SYSCHK1*
Company   Terratech
             19817 61st Ave. S.E.
             Snohomish, WA 98290
Type   Shareware
             donation requested

SYSCHK1.ARC is the distributed file and contains SYSCHK.EXE and SYSCHK.DOC. The program performs checksums of the first and second files in the root directory and the COMSPEC file. These, of course, are usually the three most important system files. The first time the program is invoked, the checksums are displayed. You can then record those values. If the program is then run with the checksum for the file given as a parameter, it's compared against the current value. Error levels are set so a batch file can test the results. A simple (and not totally effective) approach.

SoftSafe

Product   *SoftSafe*
Company   Software Directions, Inc.
             1572 Sussex Turnpike
             Randolph, NJ 07869
             (800) 346-7638
Type   Commercial
             $99

SoftSafe provides more than just virus protection; it's also a means of insuring data security for personal computers. This includes preventing unauthorized viewing, copying, modifying,

or destruction of your valuable data, as well as offering power-
ful virus protection, according to the manufacturer, Software
Directions, Inc. (who also makes the printer control program,
PrintQ).

"The primary objective in *SoftSafe*'s design is ease of use,"
said Geoffrey Wiener, president of SD.

SoftSafe gives you password protection of your hard disk,
allowing one "owner" to create up to seven authorized "users"
for each PC. The owner can also delete users or change any
password, and users can change their own password at any
time.

Interruptions are no longer a problem when working with
sensitive data. *SoftSafe*'s lockout feature allows you to hit a hot
key sequence to cover the entire screen with the *SoftSafe* password display. Then, only your password unlocks the machine,
protecting your data from unauthorized access. *SoftSafe* automatically encrypts data in designated subdirectories, so only the
user who generated the file or the computer owner can access
the files.

Finally, of course, *SoftSafe* provides powerful virus protection for your PC. *SoftSafe* maintains a protected copy of the
critical system files and compares these to the working files
each time you boot up. If *SoftSafe* detects tampering, it gives
you the option of replacing the infected files with a clean copy,
or ignoring the change if it was intentional, such as with a DOS
version upgrade.

SoftSafe works on IBM PC XT/AT and 100 percent compatibles including the PS/2. The list price of $99 includes
floppy disk and a manual, as well as 30 days free technical
support.

Tracer

Product   *Tracer* Virus Detector
Company   InterPath
          4423 Cheeney Street
          Santa Clara, CA 95054
          (408) 988-3832
Type   Commercial
          $49.95

Tracer is a computer virus detection system that catches viruses which enter your system. It uses, according to the documentation, a high reliability detection mechanism that monitors all system areas susceptible to viral attacks. If a virus does enter your system, *Tracer* will identify the specific system area or program files that have been infected, so virus removal is simplified.

There are two phases of operation for *Tracer*. The initial install phase logs the system's hardware and software parameters—including the initial interrupt vector states, boot sector instructions, hidden DOS files, device drivers, and all executable code on the hard disks. Initial load instructions, branch addresses, and other program states are also logged for each program on the hard disk. The subsequent check phase executes each time the system is powered on or rebooted, and it checks all system parameters for tracers of infection.

Tracer is designed to detect all types of viruses, including boot sector infectors and embedded viruses (viruses that leave the infected program's size and external indicators unchanged). It provides, says its manufacturer, "a timely and near foolproof indication of infection.

Trojan Stop

Product   *Trojan Stop Deluxe* version 1.1
Company   Carey Nash
          The Programmer's Forum
Type   Freeware
          Available in IBMSW on CompuServe

"*Trojan Stop Deluxe,*" writes Carey Nash in the documentation included with this freeware offering, "is a program I wrote while learning assembly. It can successfully stop any attempt to do harmful damage to your hard disk or floppy disk system. If you suspect a program is a Trojan, all you have to do is load STOP.COM before you run it."

Trojan Stop Deluxe works by hooking onto interrupt 13 hex. Interrupt 13 is used for all low-level disk I/O, and any program that accesses the disk must use it. STOP.COM monitors interrupt 13 and checks to see which function is being requested: read, write, or format. If write or format is requested, STOP.COM does not allow interrupt 13 to perform the command; instead it returns a value to tell the calling program that the write, or format was successful. It will also place a colored square on the upper right corner of your screen.

Here's an example from the documentation that comes with *Trojan Stop Deluxe:*

You have a program that has little documentation and seems much too small to do what it should do. You suspect it's a Trojan. First, run STOP.COM and then proceed to run the suspected Trojan. If the program does any disk writes or formats, you'll see a little red or blue square on your screen, and the program will be disabled—however, the suspected Trojan won't know this. If the program turns out to be okay (no nasty messages after it's done or other mischief), everything is fine. However, if it turns out to be a Trojan and claims to have done harm to your disk, merely reboot your computer and you're safe!

"Stop," Carey continues, "has been tested with everything from the FORMAT command, to DEL *.*. However, I accept no responsibility for what happens to your system while STOP.COM is in memory. This is just an attempt to supply people with a way to safeguard their systems against Trojans."

Universal Viral Simulator

Product   *Universal Viral Simulator*
Company   National BBS Society
          6226 Channel Drive
          San Jose, CA 95123
          Voice (408) 727-4559, BBS (408) 988-4004
Type   Commercial
          This program is made available to universities and
          government research organizations and on a limited
          basis to appropriate divisions within private in-
          dustry. To apply for access, see the above address.

The *Universal Viral Simulator* is a program that simulates
characteristic activities that .COM and .EXE infector viruses
use for replication. It also simulates some of the destructive
activities used by viruses to destroy disk information. It does
not simulate the infection techniques of boot infector viruses
(such as the Pakistani Brain Virus).

The *Universal Viral Simulator* is *not* a virus protection
program; it's meant to be used as a tool to test the effectiveness
of antiviral measures and as a demonstration tool for viral
replication activities.

"The use of live viruses for testing the security of individual or multiple system installations is extremely impractical,"
said Tim McCurry, technology director for the Society. "If the
security system failed during the testing/assurance process, the
results could be disastrous. Clearly, a noninvasive approach to
the validation of in-house antiviral systems and off the shelf
products is needed."

The viral simulator is executed after any antiviral systems
have been loaded and activated. It then attempts to infect the
system in a variety of different ways. Each time it's blocked by
the antiviral system, an appropriate message is displayed, naming the replication attempt technique and the fact that the attempt was unsuccessful. Likewise, if the simulator is successful
in "infecting" the system, it will identify the procedure it used
to "fool" the antiviral system.

The pseudo-virus will also simulate events typical of a virus that has activated and is attempting to destroy or disable
system data. The *Universal Viral Simulator* is nondestructive
and has no permanent effect on the system.

Vaccine from FoundationWare

Product   *Vaccine*
Company Mike Riemer
         FoundationWare
         2135 Renrock
         Cleveland, OH 44118
         (800) 722-8737
Type   Commercial
         $189

    Vaccine from FoundationWare (as distinct from the similarly-named *Vaccine from World Wide Data* below, and several public domain programs of the same name) is a sophisticated, top-end viral protection software. It's especially appropriate for networked computers. When *Vaccine* is installed on your hard disk, it continually tests files for the presence of any viruses, without the interruption of your computer's operation. If a *Vaccine* detects a virus, it will prevent the virus from damaging your system while alerting you to the danger.

    Vaccine also protects against bombs. The second a bomb tries to override the operating system with an illegal "write to disk" command, *Vaccine* halts the process and flashes you a warning. *Vaccine* can even electronically remove your hard disk from the rest of the system and provide a safe area for testing dubious software.

    Bugs are also caught. Bugs, of course, are those unintentional little things that go wrong with software after prolonged use. They also result from power surges, static electricity, and other often unexplained causes. Bugs often aren't as destructive as viruses, but commonly disrupt the integrity of your data.

    You probably don't want many people playing with your computers. If for no other reason, employees using software not approved by the company waste valuable corporate resources. *Vaccine* is designed to allow the system manager to control what software can exist and be utilized on a system, thus disallowing any unapproved software to run. This helps to standardize software and training within an organization and keeps people from playing games on your computers.

For additional usage control, *Vaccine* has a tracking feature that enables you to monitor what software has been run on your system and when. You can also install *Vaccine* to aid in determining the source of a virus (even if you approve an infected program).

Vaccine also reduces human error and recovers damaged or lost data. Again, this is sophisticated software. You may obtain additional information on it by calling the toll-free number listed above.

Vaccine from World Wide Data

Product   *Vaccine* 2.1
Company Ron Benvenisti
               World Wide Data Corp.
               17 Battery Place
               New York, NY 10004
               (212) 422-4100
Type   Commercial
               $79.95 ($25 site licensing)

Vaccine is a software viral protection package consisting of the *Vaccine* program, and two other utilities, *Antidote* and *Checkup*.

Antidote scans your disk for all viruses known to World Wide Data. It then notifies you if any of them appear to have attacked any of your programs. *Checkup* keeps a record of the state of your system and informs you if any of your executable fields (.EXE and .COM) have been changed since the last time *Checkup* was run.

Vaccine is a resident program. Once you run it, you can continue to use your system as you normally do. *Vaccine* automatically and transparently checks every exceptional situation described above. If any program you run tries to alter your system in a suspicious way, *Vaccine* warns you about what the program is trying to do and gives you the chance to stop the destructive operation.

An example given in the well-written *Vaccine User's Manual* is that of TSR programs. No memory resident program is permitted to remain in memory unless its name is declared legal to *Vaccine*. No program is permitted to perform an absolute write to any device or to modify another executable program unless the user specifically and intentionally grants it permission. Memory addresses are checked as well to prevent any virus from corrupting the programs and data in your machine.

These functions are performed in the background; thus they are transparent to the user. Once the program is loaded, the only time you see it work is when it warns you of possible danger. Trusted and approved programs that might otherwise trigger *Vaccine* are listed in an exceptions file (an ASCII file you can create with any text editor). These will include the names of all programs that change memory tables or install themselves as resident. Debuggers and communication programs, for example, often legitimately change memory tables.

There is one situation the user's manual cautions you about (and one that applies equally to *all* viral protection software). The programs you list as exceptions must be *clean* to begin with—if they've been infected with viruses that *Vaccine* does not recognize, you may not be protected from them. Any program you approve then, should be a reliable legitimate copy, generated from a known original source. This includes *Vaccine* itself. Again, this should apply to all protection programs.

Vaccine is a strong, well-programmed package already in wide use. It's well worth checking out for your own system.

Vacine

Product   *Vacine* 1.3
Company   Art Hill
           936 S. Kensington Ave.
           La Grange, IL 60525
Type   Shareware
           contribution (amount up to you)

This program, says its author Art Hill, will give you some protection against the recent crop of so-called virus programs. The program has only two modes of operation: INSTALL and CHECK. To install the program, copy it to the root directory of your hard disk. Run it by typing VACINE and selecting the appropriate option. The program works by comparing critical files to known good copies. It will record certain information it needs to check for viruses in a subdirectory on your hard disk. You may also compare critical files to those on a floppy disk. Typing VACINE C will perform the comparison against copies on your hard disk. Just typing VACINE allows you to compare to critical files on an original DOS disk.

"No doubt," Art said, "one of these low life creeps who create the virus programs will get hold of this program and figure out a way to defeat it. With your contribution I can keep upgrading the program with more and more elaborate schemes to defeat the jerks."

Despite the author's unique way of spelling "vacine" as opposed to "vaccine," the program appears to run well and is worth looking at. Its viral protection is limited to file comparison, but should be an important part of your overall system defenses.

V_Check

Product   *V_Check* 1.0
Company Dave Millis
                P.O. Box 2371
                Glenview, IL 60025
Type   Shareware
                $5, available in CompuServe IBMSW

V_Check Series 1.0, according to Dave Millis in the documentation supplied with the program, was written as a service for the many computer users who may be concerned about the growing number of virus programs and the destruction that can result from them.

"The inspiration for *V_Check*," Dave writes, "comes from not only the extensive reading of current computer literature, but also from my experience consulting people who work with micro computers in a university setting. Software needs to be protected, but not everyone can afford a commercial package, some of which can be very expensive. In fact, with the extensive network of computer users throughout the world, less expensive tools for detecting and preventing the wrath of viruses are extremely necessary. For this reason I wrote the *V_Check* program series."

V_Check is a conglomeration of six programs to do a comprehensive check on your important files and on DOS system files. The programs supplied in the archived distribution file are:

SCC.COM. Run this first. This program compares date, time, size and checksum of system files against an original copy in the A: or B: drive.

SFC.COM creates a hidden file with date, time, and size of system files if one does not exist. On successive runs, it checks this information against the current status of the file.

MCF.COM creates a database of information (in a hidden file) that contains time, date, size, and checksum for each file entered.

CCF.COM uses the data file created by MCF.COM and runs a check on the current status of the files, making sure there are no changes to time, date, size or checksum.

DSFC.COM deletes the hidden file created by SFC.COM.

DMCF.COM deletes the hidden file created by MCF.COM.

In these times, continues the *V_Check* documentation, when more and more people are offering protection from viruses, *V_Check* programs offer detection of viruses that change a file's time, date, size or checksum.

"Although some other programs offer much of the same as *V_Check*," Dave continues, "I have tried to produce a much more complete set of programs and have also made the source code available for those who would like to customize or personalize the routines for either special additions or other purposes.

"I have had a lot of people try out *V_Check* and tell me what they thought of it. (Of course, more feedback and suggestions are always welcome.) Having been tested on a large number of IBM and IBM compatible computers, incorporating at least ten different types of DOS, both PC-DOS and MS-DOS, I have not found an MS type DOS that could not be checked with *V_Check*.

"However, I offer *V_Check* as is and make absolutely no guarantees implied or otherwise. If used as recommended, *V_Check* Series 1.0 will hopefully help people detect and eliminate viruses infecting computers which result in costly damage."

WPHD.COM

Product   *WPHD* (Write Protect Hard Disk)
Type   Unattributed Public Domain
            free
            available in Delphi Writers Group,
            CompuServe IBMSW, and numerous other places

This little gem will write- and format-protect your hard disks. Run once it protects, run it again it unprotects.

Run this to write- and format-protect your hard disk. It's useful when you let someone else use your PC or try out new BBS software. Each time it's run, it toggles the protection off or on—no need to reboot to get rid of it. The toggle on/off feature will not work if, after running *WPHD,* you run another resident program that revectors INT 13. In other words, run *WPHD* after running other resident programs, such as *Sidekick.*

If the DOS FORMAT command is run when this is on, it will appear to be formatting your hard disk, but it's actually VERIFYing each sector, which does not harm the disk. Your data is actually lost during a format when DOS writes a new Directory and FAT—*WPHD* will prevent that. Actually, if *WPHD* is not installed and you accidentally start formatting your hard disk, you can type Ctrl-Break to stop the formatting. The Ctrl-Break will not be acknowledged right away, but that's all right—it will still break you out of format before any damage is done. This one is *highly* recommended. Get it and use it.

XFICHECK

Product   *XFICHECK* 4.0
Company   Chuck Gilmore
          Gilmore Systems
          P.O. Box 3831
          Beverly Hills, CA 90212-0831
          Voice: (213) 275-8006 BBS: (213) 276-5263
Type   Shareware
          Extended version of *FICHECK,* free to registered
          users

When you register your copy of *FICHECK* with Gilmore Systems (see *FICHECK*), they will send you not only guaranteed, virus-free copies of *FICHECK* and *MFICHECK,* but *XFICHECK* as well. *XFICHECK* (eXtended FICHECK) incorporates both CRC and MCRC checking in a single pass, and doesn't take much longer to run than *MFICHECK.* The added security and peace of mind of dual-checking for CRC and MCRC alone is worth the registration fee, but that's not all *XFICHECK* does. *XFICHECK* does everything *FICHECK* and *MFICHECK* do together, and more.

XFICHECK, like *FICHECK* and *MFICHECK* can only be run from a system that was booted from a DOS floppy. However, some people simply don't want to bother taking the extra precaution of booting from a floppy. Although the company does not endorse the practice, *XFICHECK* comes with information explaining how to defeat the check so you may run the program without actually booting DOS from a floppy.

9
MACINTOSH

The rotten apple injures its neighbour.

Chaucer

The Macintosh has been beset with viruses for at least the past two years. The Scores virus (see its description in Chapter 2) was first reported in 1987, and it's still out there and still causing trouble.

Viruses get into Macintosh systems disguised as *Hyper-Card* stacks or applications. The virus is self-replicating and thus spreads from machine to machine. They can (and do) infect such Macintosh resources as INITs and CODE. A well-designed virus infects other systems and attempts to hide code in as many carriers or Trojan horses as possible.

A virus, in the end, is eventually triggered and completes whatever tasks (usually nefarious) planned by the twisted mind that created it. This can and does include numerous things, up to and including erasing a disk on a specific date.

Computer viruses have an uncanny resemblance to biological viruses. In the Macintosh, it can spread from the carrier or Trojan (the stack or application that received it "through the door") into other places such as System files. Once entrenched, the replicated copies of the virus can lay dormant for days, weeks, months, or maybe even *years*.

If your Macintosh got infected last year and you do nothing, you may not know it until next year. Next year, however, *boy* will you know it as files disappear.

There are three major virus infestations of Macs. Two of these we've already discussed in the course of this book—the Scores and the Peace virus from *MacMag*. The latter bears the "honor" of being the first virus to infect commercial shrink-wrapped software, Aldus' *FreeHand* (see "How Safe Can You Be?" in Chapter 4).

In this chapter we introduce the third type of Macintosh-specific virus and discuss some ways to avoid or purge viruses in and from your system. We'll also look at some of the viral protection tools available for Macintosh computers and take a look at the virus problem on other Apple computers as well.

nVIR

The major Macintosh virus not yet discussed is called *nVIR*. While it doesn't have the fame of Scores and the Peace virus, it's out there. One sign of its presence is beep infected programs make when you start them.

In the same manner as Scores—reports Kristi Coale in her excellent article about viruses in the September, 1988 *MacUser*—nVIR installs its own code segments into an application's resources. Each time you call the application after that, the nVIR virus resources are also installed. The code searches the System folder for its INIT, and should this not be there, it will copy it to the System folder and include nVIR resources 0–7.

After the virus has established itself, it will then infect applications through its INIT (ID = 32). This virus will also add CODE ID = 256 as a resource. Here's one procedure for getting rid of nVIR infection. It comes from Chris Borton at the University of California at San Diego (USCD) and is available on many of the computer networks, including CompuServe. A good knowledge of how to use *ResEdit* is required.

First, open INIT 32 in your System File with *ResEdit*. Next, select all hex code and delete. Enter in two bytes—4E 75—which merely puts an RTS there. Go into each nVIR resource and delete all information in them. Don't delete those resources! The virus checks for their existence (only); if they are there, it assumes they're okay. With the changes above, they are harmless and won't spread the virus further.

The virus depends upon INIT 32 and nVIR 0–7 resources in the System file. It modifies the CODE #0 resource to each application, altering eight bytes in the jump table to execute the code in CODE #256, which it also installs. The nVIR resources hold copies of important information—#2 has the eight original bytes from the applications CODE 0 resource. #6 is a copy of

INIT 32, and so on. The eight bytes are the first eight on the third line in *ResEdit.*

For those who might not be that comfortable with *ResEdit,* Mike Scanlin has written *VirusWarningINIT* and *Vaccination.* The first is a virus alarm that goes off whenever one of the nVIR resources are found, or if the nVIR CODE segment is detected. The second program, *Vaccination,* looks for nVIR and reports on the status of an application. It also acts to prevent nVIR from infecting your system in the first place.

Mike's programs are distributed as the "stuffed" file VACCIN.SIT in the Macintosh area (Personal) on CompuServe.

Virus RX

Apple, like the other major players in the computer hardware and software business, remained markedly silent on the subject of viruses for a long time. Unlike the others, however, Apple did finally react to the pleas of their customers—especially after they were hit themselves with the Scores virus in at least their Washington office (according to an AP report—see Chapter 2).

First, Apple called in the FBI. This writer talked with a number of people who thought the perpetrator of the Scores virus would soon be brought to justice, but no one would say anything for publication. (Let's hope the slimebucket finds out that justice is not blind after all).

Second, Apple is providing a program, *Virus RX,* free along with guidelines on how to use it. This is, says Apple, "a public service."

Virus RX, according to the documentation Apple supplies with it, will list damaged applications, INIT, cdev and RDEV files, invisible files, altered system files, and altered applications. The program reports different levels of concern, from simple comments to dangerous to fatal.

Damaged applications are the first to be listed. These have not been infected by the virus, but they will not work and should probably be removed from your disk. The program next lists all INIT, cdev, and RDEV files (such as the Easy Access, Mouse or AppleShare files) in your System Folder. Many of these are common, but you should make sure you know why they're on your disks. Some files are normally invisible; *Virus Rx* checks these and lists them. The documentation continues, explaining how to determine if you have a virus and how to remove the infection.

Virus RX is available free on Delphi, CompuServe, other networks, various computer bulletin boards, and through your local Apple dealer. It's designed primarily for the Scores virus. Below is more detailed information on killing Scores.

Killing the Scores Virus

The following information on the Scores virus was written and provided to the public domain by Howard Upchurch, a Macintosh computer consultant in Garland, Texas and distributed by the Mac Pack and the Dallas Apple Corps for all members of the Macintosh community. Mr. Upchurch gives special thanks to John Cail, Doug Ruddman, Kelly and Cheney Coker, and Steve Schroader for their assistance. It's reprinted here with Howard's kind permission.

Introduction. A virus is an organism that attacks and feeds off a host until either the virus or the host dies. A so-called Scores virus has spread throughout the Macintosh community. This virus, however, is a nasty piece of software written by a demented individual. Just like a living organism, it reproduces itself and has spread like an epidemic. Rumors (and there are *plenty!*) are that thousands of U.S. Government Macintoshes including those owned by NASA are infected, and that the FBI is investigating the outbreak.

In addition, Apple, other major corporations, and probably hundreds of thousands of business and private users are infected. This is not the *MacMag* virus, which was relatively benign and was inadvertently spread by Aldus in a few copies of *FreeHand*. It is not the nVIR virus, which so far has spread very little, according to published sources. It *is* a virus that was purposely designed to spread itself as rapidly as possible. Scores will enter a disk as part of an application. It will spread to the System, then to other applications, some of which will be given to a friend or taken to work, spreading it even further.

There is evidence that it can spread through a network. Scores will damage programs, causing unpredictable problems. Its primary intent has not yet been discerned. Don't be the first to discover the evil purpose for which this virus was designed. Get it out of all systems in which it is located, and do it *now!*

Detection: Open the System Folder on all disks in your possession, especially hard disks. Look for two icons representing the Scrapbook File and Note Pad File. The System is infected if *both* of them are there *and* if both icons are generic document icons—for example, blank dog-eared pages. The System is probably not infected if neither or only one icon is present or if the icons look like Macintoshes, the same icon used for the System and Finder.

If the disk is infected, don't panic. The information below tells how to remove the virus from the System and prevent its recurrence. If the disk is not infected, learn here how to protect yourself and to help someone else remove the virus.

Macintosh programs used to perform productive tasks are called applications. Common applications are *MacWrite, MacPaint,* and *Microsoft Word.* Other applications with which everyone is familiar are the *Font/ DA Mover, HyperCard,* and *TeachText.* Many users don't realize that the Finder is also an application.

Items created by applications are called *documents.* A letter created with *MacWrite,* for instance, is a document. There are other items on a Mac like System and General, which are neither applications nor documents. These items, along with applications and documents, may be termed files. Generically, any item that has an icon on a Macintosh is called a *file.*

Macintosh files are composed of smaller groups of software called resources and data. Thus any Macintosh file may contain data, resources, or both. An application is comprised primarily of resources; a document is comprised primarily of data.

137

Resources with which everyone is familiar are fonts and icons. Others of importance to this discussion are CODE and INITs. CODE is contained in virtually every application, for it's really the heart of the application itself. CODE is the set of commands that controls all the other resources. An INIT is a set of instructions loaded into the Mac's memory when power is turned on and a disk is inserted. INITs are executed in alphabetical order.

Common INITs are Suitcase and Pyro. Apple has provided an application called the *Resource Editor,* ResEdit, or ResEd for short. It is a necessary tool for both identification and removal of this virus, but it is quite powerful and beginners are urged to avoid any uses of this program other than those described here.

Analysis of Infected Application. The Scores virus seems to attack only files that have CODE resources, primarily applications. Although it's possible for documents to contain CODE, no specific examples are known. It should be mentioned that files that have been stored in the Stuffit format contain no resources at all, so a file saved or archived in that manner should be impervious to infection IF it was clean when Stuffed.

Effects of Using an Infected Application. When an infected application is opened, its new CODE commands tell it to add several new pieces of software to the System Folder. The Scrapbook File and Note Pad File are quite important because they provide the best clue that something is wrong.

The virus makes other changes to the System Folder that are less obvious: It adds a Desktop file and a file called Scores, from which the virus gets its name. These files cannot be observed from the Finder because they're invisible. Programs such as *ResEd* and *Mac-Tools* show them to be there, however.

The virus also modifies the System itself, adding the following resources: atpl ID 128, DATA ID-4001, and INITs with IDs of 10, 6, and 17. With these new INIT resources in the System, the Mac is figuratively a fused bomb, ready to do damage the next time it's turned on.

Spread of Virus to Uncontaminated Applications. Because these new resources are primarily INITs, they are activated the next time the Mac is started. Once initialized, the virus begins to execute the commands that cause it to spread. As the infected disk is used, the virus continually seeks uncontaminated applications. The present thought is that it searches in a random fashion at an interval of three and a half minutes. At times a disk drive will begin operating when nothing should be happening. This occurs because the virus is writing its code resource to another application. After a long enough period of time, every application on the disk will be infected, apparently whether it has been used or not.

Prevention of Occurrence or Recurrence. CE Software has released into the public domain a utility called *Vaccine*. *Vaccine* is a "cdev," which means "Control Panel Device." Copies are free. Get it from a Disk-of-the-Month (DOM) at a user group meeting or from a telephone communication service such as Compu-Serve, Delphi, or GEnie.

To use it, place the *Vaccine* icon in the System Folder. Select Control Panel from the Apple menu and you'll see *Vaccine* listed right under General. Close examination will reveal that the name begins with a space before the "V." Leave it that way so it will be the first thing that operates when the Mac is started or reset. Select the *Vaccine* icon and read the instructions.

In case you don't understand them, putting an X in the top and bottom boxes is recommended. Be sure to restart the Mac after setting *Vaccine* in order to start it working. To help assure you have a clean copy of *Vaccine,* select the *Vaccine* icon while at the Finder (not the Control Panel) and choose Get Info from the File menu. Verify that the size is 11,875 bytes and that the creation date is Saturday, March 19, 1988 at 11:49 p.m. We must assure that no one creates a bogus version of this fine work. And thank you, CE Software!

After *Vaccine* has been installed, look for the following symptoms when using the Mac or opening an application; each is an indication that the virus is in operation:

1. Vaccine randomly asks for permission to alter a resource.
2. Opening an application triggers *Vaccine.*
3. Opening a resource causes a bomb (usually ID = 02).
4. Opening an application causes the Mac to hang up.

Do not put a copy of any application on a hard disk until it has been checked for contamination. Do not run a new copy of any program until it has been checked out. Examine any program before uploading it to a Bulletin Board.

Removal of Virus from System. Since the relatively recent discovery of this virus, several programmers are working on developing software that will do any or all of the following: detect the presence of the virus, remove it from the System Folder, detect infected applications, and/or repair the infected applications. As of this writing, however, none are available. What follows is a step-by-step procedure that will enable you to clean up a disk with or without one or more of these utility programs.

First, install the *Vaccine* utility if it's available and reboot the Mac. (Note: If you see a bomb, a hangup, or a message from *Vaccine* when booting, the Finder is contaminated. Boot with a clean floppy and replace the Finder on the virused disk.) Open *ResEd.* (Note: If you see a bomb, a hangup, or a message from *Vaccine* when trying to open *ResEd, ResEd* itself is contaminated; replace it with a clean copy.) At this point you'll see the files at the so-called root level of the disk.

Notice the file called DeskTop. This is *not* the bad file. Scroll through the window and open the System Folder by double clicking on its name.

Select the Desktop file by clicking on it one time; then choose Clear from the Edit menu. Do the same thing for the other three infection files, Note Pad File,

Scores, and Scrapbook File. Locate the System and double click on its name to open it.

Locate atpl and open it by double clicking. Select atpl ID 128 and Clear it by using the Clear command under the Edit menu. Close atpl and open DATA. Clear DATA ID-4001. Close it and open INIT. Clear ID 10, ID 17, and ID 6. Close all windows except the root level window and save the changes when asked if you wish to.

Important: A virgin System (4.1, at least) from Apple does not contain either resource of the types atpl or DATA, but some programs, *LaserSpeed,* for one, legitimately place them in the System. Remove only the ID numbers listed.

The System is now free of infection, but the work is far from over. When *Vaccine* has been properly installed on the disk, opening an infected application will cause either a bomb or a message from *Vaccine.* The Mac may also hang up.

In any case, the application should be examined more closely: Use *ResEd* to open the CODE resource of the suspected application. If the top CODE ID is two numbers higher than the next highest, Get Info on it. If the size is 7026, it is an infected application. Throw it in the trash because it's unusable and will reinstall the virus into the System if it is run with *Vaccine* off or not installed.

Even if you don't yet have a copy of *Vaccine,* use *ResEd* to examine every application on your disks. Check *all* of the applications in the manner described above. It's easy to overlook some of the smaller and perhaps lesser used ones like Font/DA Mover and backup programs.

Remember, the Finder is an application. And an application doesn't have to be run to be contaminated. Experiences with this virus over the past four months have shown this to be an effective and relatively simple way to clean a disk. There's nothing wrong with replacing the System, replacing the System Folder, or re-initializing the hard drive. These, however, are extreme measures and are not considered by the author (for example, Howard Upchurch) to be necessary.

In any case, make sure with *ResEd* that all applications put back on the hard drive are clean, especially if *Vaccine* has not yet been installed. Otherwise, the whole cycle could begin again. For more advanced users: After it's felt that all infected applications have been removed and replaced, run *Disk Express,* if available, with the Erase Free Space option turned on. This will cluster the data to the start of the disk and zero out all remaining space.

Then use *Fedit, MacTools,* or a similar program to search for two strings virtually unique to this virus: VULT and ERIC. Each string is all caps. If these strings are nowhere on the disk, it's clean. If they're still there, do everything possible to find out which file they're in and remove it from the disk. Repeat this until there is no ERIC or VULT. (The only application so far discovered that contains the VULT string is one called DD Editor, and it does not contain ERIC).

Searching a previously infected disk in this manner without running Disk Express first does no good because the infected files weren't actually erased when trashed; the remnants are probably still on the disk. In other words, the presence of ERIC and VULT at this stage of the removal process does not mean the disk is still infected, but their absence DOES mean the disk is clean.

Removal of Virus from Infected Applications. Unfortunately, at this time there is no known method to repair infected applications, and perhaps there never will be. There is evidence that when the virus attaches itself to an application and inserts the new CODE resource, at least a part of the new CODE is apparently written over some part of the original application software, permanently destroying it. If true, this would account for the many strange effects of the virus because the missing code would be different in each application.

There would have to be a separate fix for every

application. The safest thing to do is trash every bad application from the disk and replace it with a known clean copy. If there is no clean copy backed up, save the infected version on a floppy in hopes that a fix will be found.

Comments. Cleaning the virus from one disk will not fix the problem. ALL Macintosh disks must be clean or the problem will be around for a long, long time. And not just *your* disks: EVERYONE'S disks! After you're familiar with the problem and its solution, share your knowledge.

"Why am I taking the time to create this document?" writes Howard Upchurch. "I had the virus as early as November of 1987, but dismissed the problem as an offshoot of MultiFinder, due to the fact that the virus struck me just as I had decided to quit using MultiFinder and return to using System 4.1.

"I spent many hours of work over several weeks figuring it out and ridding myself of its effects. At the time I did not recognize it as a virus, and for that I am very sorry. I should have pounded on Apple's doors relentlessly asking about this problem.

"Possibly someone there would have recognized it for what it was, early enough to prevent the present massive outbreak of the problem. I have enjoyed my Mac for well over four years now. I have created three fonts with it, one shareware and two that have actually been published. I have had fun with my Mac, and I have earned money with it. I am a member of two Macintosh clubs and have made many good friends because of this small computer.

"I can't stand by while some jerk destroys so much of my life. The time has come to repay the Mac community and this is my way. Help me. One hates to publish a phone number in a document designed for public distribution, but without it you could not relay any important information.

"I have reported information as I have found it. If there are any errors in the above, I apologize but ask not to be held responsible. Some statements may prove false or incomplete as more information comes to light.

"Please call only from 8 a.m. to 8 p.m. Central time, and only if you have found some information not in this document. Long distance callers, please leave a complete message on the answering machine if it answers, as I cannot afford to return many long distance calls.

"Both User Groups of which I am a member have access to AppleLink, a worldwide communications network operated by Apple Computer, so any new information can be relayed directly to the people at Apple who are working on solving this problem. And thanks for any help."

Howard Upchurch may be reached at 3409 O'Henry Drive, Garland, TX 75042 (214) 272-7826.

Other Apples

The Macintosh and IBM types of computers have borne the brunt of viral attacks, but older Apple machines are not totally immune either. Checking the Apple II and III area on Compu-Serve, we find the programs listed below available for Apple II owners. Alas, the Apple III seems to have been abandoned even by the virus-makers.,

Apple.Rx 1.7: This is a software virus detection program. It's listed as shareware ($20) but is not to be distributed elsewhere than CompuServe. This revision corrects one bug and adds enhancements: prints only error lines if desired, adds an automatic, hands off, check mode (for use in a queue). This requires a IIGS or a IIe or IIc with a 65802 chip or 65816 board substituted for the 65C02. Copyright 1988 by Glen Bredon.

VACCINE II: This is the latest version (1.1) of VACCINE II, a full-function Virus Analyzer and detector for the IIGS. This version adds additional checks not found in the previous version, and fixes the FINDER restart problem experienced by some users. You should destroy your previous copies of VAC-CINE after download.

ANTIVI.BQY: Checks for virus on the boot block (block 0) of any ProDOS disk. Unpack with BLU to get program and documentation.

10
ATARI

Raise no more spirits than you can conjure down.

Old Proverb

Atari is no more immune from viruses than are IBM and Macintosh. Both the older 8-bit machines and the newer STs have been struck by viruses.

The ST appears to have been the hardest hit. Two ST-specific viruses have already been identified, and more are suspected. The worst of these, according to John Jainschigg writing in the September/October 1988 issue of *Atari Explorer*, seems to have originated in West Germany. The ST is very popular in that country.

This viral beastie has been named the Boot Sector virus because it inhabits the boot sector on auto-booting disks. Should an infected disk be used to initialize an ST system, the virus loads itself into memory and attaches itself to a system call vector that is related to disk access. By doing this, it can infect other appropriately configured disks whenever an access call is made.

The procedure used by this virus is to first check the disk for its own presence. If no clone of the virus exists, it makes a copy of itself into the boot sector. In such manner, the virus can be spread easily from machine to machine. When the virus decides it has replicated enough, it goes active and corrupts the File Allocation Tables (FAT) of however many floppies are put into the ST during an operating session.

The other known ST virus is somewhat less destructive. It also lives in the boot sector of autobooting disks. Its active life consists of simulating memory errors like you might expect to see if some of your computer's memory chips had become defective. This virus is not very amusing if you go to the considerable expense of replacing chips only to find (seemingly) that you still have the *same problem.*

Fighting ST Viruses

ST viruses (and 8-bit too) are spread by the exchange of infected auto-booting disks. This affects user groups much more than isolated users, since user groups do a lot of disk trading. One user who found this out, to his dismay, is Gerd Sender of Koeln, West Germany. Herr Sender was kind enough to pass along his experiences to the global community of Atari users via a text file that's been posted on numerous bulletin boards worldwide, and the full text is available in the Atari special interest group on CompuServe. Here's an excerpt from that file.

"This weekend I received a number of pd software disks from a computer store. I found that three of these contained the ST Virus that has been mentioned on the net recently. I did not however discover this until it had trashed one disk and infected a very large number of disks.

"I have since disassembled the virus and worked out exactly what it does and I am posting a summary of what I found here.

"When the ST is reset or switched on, it reads some information from track 0 sector 0 of the disk in drive A. It is possible to set up that sector so that the ST will execute its contents. The virus program is written into this sector so that it is loaded whenever the ST is booted on the offending disk.

"Once loaded into memory, the virus locates itself at the end of the system disk buffer (address contained at 0x4c2 I think) and attaches itself to the bios getbpb( ) function.

"Every time getbpb( ) is called, the virus is activated. It tests the disk to see if it contains the virus. If it doesn't then the virus is written out to the boot sector and a counter is initialized.

"If the disk does contain the virus, then the counter is incremented. Once the counter reaches a certain value, random data is written across the root directory & FAT tables for the disk, thus making it unusable. The virus then removes itself from the boot sector of the damaged disk (destroys the evidence?).

"Once the virus is installed in the ST it will copy itself to EVERY non–write-protected disk you use—EVEN IF YOU ONLY DO A DIRECTORY—or open a window to it from the desktop.

"The virus CANNOT copy itself to a write-protected disk.

"I think (but am not certain) that it survives a reset.

"The current virus does not affect hard disks (it uses the flopwr( ) call). However, if you are using an auto-boot hard disk such as Supra, and the disk in drive A contains the virus, THE FLOPPY BOOT SECTOR IS EXECUTED BEFORE THE HARD DISK BOOT SECTOR and consequently the virus will still be loaded and transferred to every floppy you use.

"To test for the virus, look at sector 0 of a floppy with a disk editor. If the boot sector is executable, it will contain 60 hex as its first byte. Note that a number of games have executable boot sectors as part of their loading. However, if this is the case, they should not load when infected by the virus.

"If people are worried about this and haven't been able to get the other killer (I have not seen it yet) then I will post the source/object for a simple virus detector/killer that I have written.

"It would appear that this virus is not the end of the story. I have heard that there is a new virus around. This one is almost impossible to detect. For each disk inserted, it scans for any *.prg and appends itself to the text segment in some way. Thus, it is very difficult to tell whether or not the virus is actually on a disk."

8-Bits Take Hits

Nor, of course, do the older Atari models get off scot-free. Portland (Oregon) Atari Club president, Bill Pike, warns Atari users of a virus that, different from ST boot sector viruses, can actually attach itself to application programs.

Writing in the widely published electronic version of the PAC newsletter, he says that an original program may run fine the first time. Yet, unknown to you, the file is a Trojan horse that lets the virus write a program to the disk.

Like some fat, crafty spider, the virus sets inside the computer memory and waits for a disk Input/Output operation.

Each time a disk is placed in the drive and an Input/Output operation is performed, a copy of the virus is written to the disk. If a file containing the virus is transferred to a BBS, the virus goes along with the program.

The virus then sets in wait on the disk. As Bill reminds us in his article, its not listed in the directory and may or may not change the VTOC. Later, at some predetermined time, the virus goes to work and may wipe out the directory and VTOC or it just might *format* the entire disk. Some virus programs modify DOS so the virus program is appended to every file on the disk when a file is loaded off of disk or transferred via modem.

Bill also says boot sector viruses exist that prey on 8-bit machines too, but Atari owners have a big advantage over other types of computers since the disk drive is a "smart-drive." This means if the disk is write-protected the drive will not write to or format that disk.

"This is part of the ROM instructions within the drive itself," Pike writes, "and a virus cannot modify ROM. However there is a modification available to bypass this feature. I would suggest that it be removed for obvious reasons."

He continues to point out that keeping the virus out of your library is much easier than removing it when it already exists. You can never be sure you've caught every disk the virus has infected. If all infected disks aren't destroyed, the virus will simply reinfect all of your disks.

Here are three basic rules of protecting yourself from viruses while using an Atari computer:

1. Disks that aren't supposed to be written to should be write-protected. It's easy enough, should you need to put something on the disk, to remove the write-protect tab and then replace it. It's better to be safe than sorry.
2. A cold start removes a virus from memory. Turn the computer off, then reboot it with a *known* good DOS disk. You should always have a good, pristine backup of the DOS disk—write-protected and never used except to make copies.
3. If you trade programs or download them from bulletin boards, keep these on a separate disk. After trying them out, do a cold boot of your computer as described above.

Finally, here's a method suggested by Bill Pike for checking out new programs:

Format a blank disk, using a known good copy of DOS. Then use a sector editor to check the first 4 sectors (0–3) of the suspect disk against the freshly formatted disk. If these don't match, one of the files on the disk has a virus. You can find the infected file by using a known good DOS and copying each file individually to another disk and comparing the boot sectors (0–3) with the newly formatted disk. You might also wish to compare all file lengths including the DOS.SYS and DUP.SYS files. If any file is longer than the original file, suspect a virus.

Conclusion

So far, the best protection against viruses on either an ST or 8-bit Atari seems to be simply to use the write-protect tab. There are a few public domain antiviral programs for Atari beginning to appear, also.

One gets the feeling that the Atari community is where the IBM and Macintosh were last year. Rumors are flying and actual infestations are appearing, but viruses are not yet as widespread as they are on IBM and compatibles, and on the Macintosh.

Alas, Atari's time seems to be coming, just like the others.

11
AMIGA

These are called the pious frauds of friendship.
Henry Fielding (1707-1754)

Commodore's Amiga computers are mighty machines, yet one little program entering in the guise of friendship can lay them low.

One of the first Amiga viruses was widely reported in October 1987 by Pete Goodeve and others on various networks and computer bulletin boards. This particular virus seems to be relatively innocuous, merely popping a message up on your screen. However, it doesn't show itself until a number of your disks are infected. Goodeve posted a message on GEnie on October 15, 1987 in which he details having seen the virus the previous evening at the Winners Circle User Group meeting.

The virus works like this: When a warm boot (Ctrl-Amiga-Amiga) is done from an infected disk, the virus writes itself into memory. Subsequent warm boots will not delete it. After that, until such time as power has been removed from the machine, other disks placed into the computer have the virus written to their boot sectors, and will pass the infection on in the same manner.

The message this virus throws onto the screen, as best Pete could remember, was:

"Something wonderful has happened—Your Amiga is alive! And what is more, some of your disks are infected by a virus! Brought to you by [something . . . something] SCA."

Apparently this virus was meant to be benign. However, it may have spread to thousands of Amiga computers, disrupting the normal operating parameters of these machines. A report about this virus in CompuServe's *Online Today* pointed out that some commercial software developers use coded information in the boot block of their distribution disks. In such cases the virus can inadvertently damage these disks and render the software useless. The virus was evidently meant to be a high-tech joke, displaying the message above after having invaded and entrenched itself in a user's disk library.

Like the supposedly benign Macintosh Peace virus, this Amiga infestation at the very least caused a lot of users consternation. None of us want *anyone* messing with our precious disks.

Viruses Go South for the Winter

After October 1987, the next major virus outbreak in the Amiga community occurred in sunny Florida during January 1988. A United Press International report quotes members of the Tampa Amiga User's Group as saying they were engaged in a fight against viruses. One person said the virus was set to start destroying files on May 13th (see the *Friday the 13th* virus described in Chapter 2).

"It kind of creeps up on you," president Jeff White of the Amiga group said to UPI, and continued to say that many of the group's membership now had disks infected by this virus.

The UPI report continued, "Experts don't yet know what, if any, damage the virus can cause to the disks or programs. Similar problems have erased programs and information. . . . White said the program spread itself to more than 20 of his floppy disks before he discovered it. But by then, the program had spread to the disks of many of the club's members via its regular disk-of-the-month distribution."

White told UPI the program works invisibly. "When the computer is turned on, the program stores itself in the machine's main memory and then begins spreading copies of itself to new disks used in the machine," he said.

He stated that Tampa Amiga User's Group members now employ a virus-checker program to test disks and prevent infections.

SCA, All the Way!

The virus discussed above also resurfaced in January 1988—now named the SCA virus. Chet Solace, Assistant Editor of the

Amiga-oriented *AMnews Magazine,* posted public warning messages on various boards saying the magazine had inadvertently spread the virus.

"If you got a copy of *AMnews,* Vol. 2, No.1 (WHITE Cover) at AMI-EXPO," reads the warning in part, "install Disk#1, using a write-protected copy of WorkBench! If you ALREADY used *AMnews,* any BOOTABLE disk used prior to POWER-OFF is also infected! Check ALL such disks/memory with VCheck19.arc. NON-BOOTABLE DISKS ARE SAFE!"

Like the Aldus *FreeHand* case and the Macintosh Peace virus, the Amiga community now had to face the fact that even commercial software was not safe from viral infection.

Solace went on to describe what had happened and the steps the magazine was taking to rectify the situation. He wrote that after the January master disks had been sent for copying, someone added the virus to Disk#1 before duplication. Through the three days of demonstrations at the show, the virus remained hidden until 300 prerelease copies had been sold.

Chet then emphasizes that no other infected copies were released and that all copies were being certified virus free and repackaged.

"Since all copies of Disk#1 had the same 'generation' of virus," he said, "it had to be done just prior to, or during copying. We've added security, and future issues will automatically check for viruses! We are stunned at this senseless violence, and apologize to all those affected for the inconvenience, aggravation and delay."

VirusX: Steve Tibbett's Virus Killer

Product   *VirusX*
Company Steve Tibbett
                  2710 Saratoga Pl. #1108
                  Gloucester, Ontario
                  K1T 1Z2
                  BBS 613-731-3419
                  BIX s.tibbett, People/Link SteveX
Type   Copyrighted, but freely distributable and not
                  shareware

Steve Tibbett's *VirusX* is one of the leading programs in virus-fighting on the Amiga, and Steve himself is a leading authority on Amiga viruses. *VirusX* has gone through several revisions (we looked at 1.7 here) and is tailored to protect against not only the SCA virus, but several others as well. The first he addresses, however, is the SCA virus.

"There are a number of CLI-based Virus Checkers out there," writes Steve in the documentation included in the archived *VirusX* distribution file, "which do their job just fine, but if you're not into using CLI, what do you do? You use *VirusX!*

"Please, I encourage you to give this program to anybody who might have the virus. Including your local dealer—some of the dealers in this area have the virus all over their disks, which they allow customers to copy, and they don't do anything about it because they don't know how. *VirusX* makes it extremely simple."

VirusX can be put in your Startup-Sequence. When run, it will open a small window so you know it's there (and it will display the occasional message in it). Whenever a disk is inserted into any of the 3½-inch drives, that disk is automatically checked for the SCA virus and is also checked to see if its boot sector is Standard.

"If the disk has a nonstandard boot sector," writes Steve, "it is either a new form of virus which I don't know about yet, or it is a commercial program which uses the boot block for something constructive (like booting their game)."

If *VirusX* finds a boot block it is suspicious about, it will present the user with a requester either warning him that the disk has the SCA virus or telling him that the boot code is nonstandard. In either case, he is given the option to either ignore it or Remove it.

If the user selects Remove, after he says he's sure he wants to rewrite the disk's boot sector, the boot code written back to the disk by *VirusX* is the same boot code that the AmigaDOS INSTALL command writes. (Remember: Never rewrite the boot sector of a commercial program unless you *know* that program doesn't use it for something else. If the program gives you the AmigaDOS window before running, you know it's safe to repair that disk.)

"If you run across a strain of the virus, or any other virus that *VirusX* doesn't specifically warn of, *please* send me a copy of a disk with that virus on it! I want to keep *VirusX* current, and to do so, I need the viruses.

"Of course, there are those of you who are thinking that I am some nut case trying to spread my own virus hidden under the guise of a virus checker. Well, just for you, I've included the C source code. Please, if you don't trust me, don't discard a useful utility as untrustworthy for no reason, CHECK THE SOURCE! Recompile it if you think I'm trying to slip a fast one on you. I just want to see the virus out of all of our lives."

The Byte Bandit Virus

Steve Tibbett's *VirusX* also goes for the throat of the Byte Bandit virus. Once it's in memory, the Byte Bandit virus copies itself to just above the high memory point on the first hunk of RAM it can find. This means it's not always in the same place. The virus wedges itself into the Interrupt Server chain, into the Trackdisk.device's vectors, and creates itself a Resident structure so it can hang around after reboot.

Byte Bandit watches every disk inserted and will write itself to any bootable disk that's inserted. This one, says Steve, can spread like wildfire. Every disk you insert into your external drive during a session with this Virus loaded will result in all those disks being infected. If you install a disk while this virus is going, it will just copy itself back to the disk.

When *VirusX* finds this virus on a disk, it will also display a Copy Count, which is the number of disks that have been infected by that Branch on the Tree that the virus is on. If you infect a disk with your copy, and your copy is number 300, that copy will be #301.

"If that one infects somebody," writes Steve, "that will be #302, but on your copy, two infestations down the line, there will be another #302. Anyway, the copy count on my Byte Bandit virus is #879. Note that *VirusX* will check RAM for this virus as well as the disk. This was necessary as you can tell from the description above.

"Special thanks must go here to Dave Hewett who, 2 days after I gave him a copy of the virus, gave me a printed, commented disassembly of the virus with meaningful labels and everything I needed to stomp it. Thanks Dave!

"Thanks must also go to Bruce Dawson of CygnusSoft Software, who went to the trouble of being the first person to send me this Virus."

The Revenge Virus

"This virus is not yet common in North America (I think I'm the first person here to have a copy of it)," says Steve Tibbett, "but it is apparently making the rounds in Sweden and Germany, so that's who this version of *VirusX* is more or less directed to. (I'm sure we'll get that virus over here soon enough!)

"What this virus does, is everything that the Byte Bandit virus does; plus, after infecting a disk, it will wait one minute after every reboot and change your mouse pointer into an image of a certain part of the male anatomy.

"I think the reason this virus is called the Revenge virus is because it looks specifically for the Byte Bandit and for the SCA Virus. If it finds either of these, it rigs that virus so that it will crash the machine unless this virus is loaded first. Note that I might be wrong about this—that's the way it looks from the disassembly, but I don't have an SCA virus here to test it with. I tried it with the Byte Bandit and it didn't seem to do anything like this—but be warned in case it pops up later or something.

"The Revenge virus stays in RAM via changing the Cool-Capture vector to point to his own code. He then intercepts the DoIO( ) call and watches for any attempts to rewrite or to read the boot block and acts accordingly. He also has an interrupt around counting VBlanks until it's time to bring up his sicko pointer.

"To get this virus out of memory is simple. Hold down the Joystick button (plug a joystick into port 2, and hold down the button while you are rebooting) and the screen will briefly turn RED during the boot, and it's out of memory. (If you hold down Joystick button and mouse button, he will half-remove himself from RAM and turn the screen Blue.)

"*VirusX* will alert you if the virus is present in RAM and will render it helpless in RAM before telling you about it. It will also report its presence on disk."

Other Amiga Viruses

The Byte Warrior virus, reports Steve Tibbett, is a lot like the Byte Bandit virus except it's not designed to hurt anything. It will start an Alarm sound if it sees another virus, but other than that, it will write itself to any disk inserted. There is also a hidden message in it, asking us to spread it around and not to erase it . . . Right.

The latest Amiga virus Steve has found is the Obelisk Softworks Crew virus (sent to him by Jason Allen Smith, who he wishes to thank). Again, Steve *wants* you to send him any Amiga viruses so he can include defenses against them in *VirusX.* Our congratulations to Steve Tibbett for the fine job he's doing.

The Clock Virus

Product   *Chronos*
Company Dave Thomas
           contact via PhilAMIGA BBS (215-533-3191)
Type   public domain

The following information on the Clock virus is supplied to the public domain by Dave Thomas along with a program to fight the virus. The program is available from the board above, or on GEnie, among other places.

As many of you are aware, writes Dave, there's a virus floating about that causes trouble by causing your battery-backed-up clock to accelerate at incredible speed. There were two solutions to this problem. One was to physically remove the battery from your clock and short the terminals. This was, shall we say, inconvenient. The second solution was a program called *Clock_Doctor,* which would correct this problem.

Now, there's a new (dare we say, mutated) clock virus that causes the exact problem. It turns off your hardware clock. When you try to load or save the time using SetClock, you receive a message stating that the hardware clock is not functioning. Don't Panic!

The first solution mentioned above will also solve this problem, but the same inconvenience exists. *Clock_Doctor* doesn't detect this condition. What is a time conscious Amigan to do?

Chronos is (I hope) a foolproof clock fixer. It corrects the conditions caused by both strains of the clock virus. To use it, simply type *Chronos* from the CLI command line. It will automatically correct any problems it detects in the clock after displaying the 15 clock registers for inspection.

After this has occurred, you'll probably need to correct the system's idea of what time it is and do a setclock opt save.

Hope this helps! If you have any questions, leave E-Mail to Dave Thomas on PhilAMIGA BBS (215-533-3191). The source to the program is included. Oh, the program is also placed in the public domain.

GEnie, Repository of Amiga Virus Information

In researching this book, we found GEnie to have the best and most extensive selection of virus-related files and programs for the Amiga. Here's a list of the files currently available in the Amiga Round Table:

No.	File Name	Type	Address	Access	Lib
4116	BOOTGEN.ARC	X	J.SHARRER	166	4
3702	CHET_SOLACE_VIRUS_TEXT	X	DEB	166	1
4432	CLKDOCTOR_2.0.ZOO	X	K.DEVAUGHN	59	4
4197	KILLVIRUS.ARC	X	NBARBER	230	4
3775	NEW_VIRUS_WARNING.ARC	X	K.DEVAUGHN	460	4
4245	SENTRY.ZOO	X	J.TRAVIS	78	4
4676	TCELL11.ARC	X	O.SIDDIQUE	40	4
3269	THE_VIRUS.TXT	X	BJACKSON	236	1
3591	VCHECK1.9.ARC	X	JSP	323	4
4011	VIEWBOOT.11.ARC	X	E.GORDON	140	4
4003	VIEWBOOT.ARC	X	GRAFIX.M	229	4
4744	VIRUSX15.ARC	X	O.SIDDIQUE	215	4
4809	VIRUSX15W.ZOO	X	E.PENNI	159	4
4645	VIRUSX_1.4.ARC	X	K.HANS	218	4
3981	WARP11Z.ZOO	X	C.HATCH	78	4
4325	PROTECTION.ARC	X	K.HANS	41	18
4165	VIRUS-CLTD	X	J.MOULTON1	125	1
3120	VIRUS.TXT	X	MIKEM	144	1
3368	VIRUSPIC.ARC	X	WALRUS	89	18
4879	VIRUSX1.71.ARC	X	K.HANS	66	4
4162	VIRUSX121.ARC	X	K.HANS	268	4

Interview with Steve Tibbett

We called Steve Tibbett's computer bulletin board in Ottawa, the capital of Canada, to verify the information on his program, *VirusX,* and to make sure he had no objection to publishing it. While online, Steve switched his BBS into chat mode, and the following interview occurred (online interviewing is *great* for a writer, since the interviewee writes all your notes for you!).

Tibbett: Just wanted to mention that Discovery Software has a program called *VIP,* a Virus protection program. Have you heard of or looked into it? Talk to Randy at Discovery Software, at 301-268-9877. The reason I mention it is that they just arranged with me to do some work on it, and I think it's going to be the best Amiga virus protection program.

The thing about *VIP* is that it will let you classify a new (as in, a virus you don't already know the name of) into a database. Whenever you check a disk, it will compare it against all the ones it knows—if it doesn't recognize it, you can add it.

Also, a main function of *VIP* is to make BACKUPs of boot blocks. You take all your commercial games, back up the boot blocks, and then even if a new virus does wipe something out, you can restore the disk.

Roberts: Sounds good, Steve. Hey, I might as well do a very quick mini-interview of you (if you don't mind) since you're on. Is that okay?

Tibbett: Sure. Typing fast comes in handy at long distance (grin).

Roberts: My phone bill must be getting really big talking to Canada. How serious do you see the virus problem in the Amiga community?

Tibbett: Well, the way I see it right now, there are a bunch of hackers/pirates over in Germany/Sweden/Holland/wherever, who are trading software back and forth and including viruses just for their own amusement. There aren't any viruses currently that go after anything but the boot block. That is, there's nothing malicious. It's certainly possible and I'm not looking forward to the day someone decides to start. There was the Byte Bandit virus which would crash your machine every five minutes or so on purpose, but at least it didn't cost you anything.

Roberts: Say, you're a great typist! So, no viruses yet that attach to or infect application programs?

Tibbett: Nope. I hear they are all the rage on the PC and on the Mac. It's just too easy with all those system files to infect them. Again, it's certainly possible on the Amiga. I've thought of a few easy ways of doing it, but I'm not going to be the one to try it.

Roberts: Right. Is there a lot of concern among users on this side of the Atlantic about viruses?

Tibbett: Well, it seems to me that over here, people are a lot different than people over there (computer users that is). Over here, it seems that there is ummm ummm (thinking)... There don't seem to be as many hard core "hackers" as there are over there. If you look at the arsenal of the typical pirate, it's very rare to see programs broken in North America. I'm not really sure why this is, but it seems that viruses and piracy go hand in hand, and piracy is certainly much more rampant over there.

Roberts: Hmmmmm... That's interesting, and not true in other brands of computers (grin), but from what I've read on Amiga, I certainly agree. How serious do you think the problem will get? Worse? Better? More malicious viruses?

Tibbett: Right now, there are six different viruses (and a couple of other ones which are just the same six with different text in them). I think that because all these viruses basically do the same thing (infect the boot block, spreading from machine to machine via the boot block) and because there are good PD programs out there to find boot block viruses (grin), and the amount of media attention given the issue seems to be helping. Sure, it's spawning MORE viruses, but since they all basically do the same thing, we know what they are and we know how to handle them. I have not seen a Trojan on the Amiga yet, no logic bombs, none of the other malicious stuff. Hopefully this says something about Amiga users in general.

Until somebody goes malicious, I don't see things getting any worse. Another 20 boot block viruses wouldn't surprise me, but wouldn't really hurt.

Roberts: Well, sounds like it's a lot better in Amiga-land than IBM. Most of the IBM-specific viruses are destructive. Do you see a commercial virus software market springing up for Amiga?

Tibbett: I hope so (grin) with me working on *VIP* Seriously, though, I think that the PD software is great, but it's not as good as what *VIP* is going to be, because *VIP* is the culmination of a lot of people's work. It's also got the advantage of advertising—meaning that . . . [Launching into a story here].

I work in a computer store. Quite often, people will drag in their hardware, and a bunch of their disks, and say "It's broken. None of my games work anymore." Those type things. I grab one of their disks, pop it into our machine, and up comes "Disk in DF0: is infected with the WHATEVER virus." These people might even have known that they had the virus, but they have no way of protecting themselves. One thing about PD software (on the Amiga) is that it usually requires that you be able to understand ARC and the Amiga-CLI which the average "Oh, I just bought it to play games" type person doesn't care about. A commercial program with a good manual is aimed at these people.

Roberts: Hey! Good stuff. What is the company developing *VIP,* and how much will it sell for, etc.?

Tibbett: *VIP* is already available from Discovery Software International, makers of some of the best Amiga software (*Arkanoid, Zoom, Marauder*). These guys have a real interest in the matter. I don't think they're just out to make a quick buck. With the Amiga market being as small as it is (less than 1 million), it seems that for a lot of applications, one company can fill the whole market. Example: *Marauder,* is about the only Amiga disk copier that went anywhere. If this were the PC market or Mac market, there'd be many of them. (Right? Are there?)

Roberts: Yes. I have almost 30 IBM packages here for review and more are coming to market. So *VIP* is sold through stores, mail order, etc.?

Tibbett: All of the above. Yes. At a reasonable price. I hear some of the PC ones are big bucks. *VIP* is $49.95 Canadian, probably $37.95 or so U.S. That's pretty reasonable.

Roberts: "Yes, and you are working on it?"

Tibbett: Right. The first release wasn't quite adequate for the job. The next release (probably 1.1) is going to have a really neat method of identifying new viruses, and will also keep a catalog database of all your commercial boot block blocks. So, with it, you can spot the brand new virus that just wiped out your *Arkanoid,* store the virus (so it can be spotted later on), and then fix your *Arkanoid.*

Roberts: Sounds great. Let's see, you're in Ottawa, right? The capital of Canada?

Tibbett: Gloucester, actually—a few minutes from Ottawa.

Roberts: How long have you been working with computers?

Tibbett: Oh, gee, when I was about 13 I was hanging out at a local CompuMart bugging them day and night about their Apple IIs and PETs.

Computers have changed a lot. It seems that for any computer to be taken seriously these days, it has to be IBM compatible, and I think that's a waste. In Europe, they don't depend on IBM compatibility. They buy the best computer for the job (or so I hear). That's why the ST and the Amiga are doing so much better over there than here. The Mac is a great machine and would have done a lot better if it wasn't for Big Blue stifling things. Same for the Amiga!

BBS System: Less than 2 minutes remaining.

Roberts: Thanks, Steve. I'll spell check this and make us both sound erudite. Bye.

Tibbett: Yes (grin), make me sound better! Okay, Ralph, been great talking to you. Looking forward to seeing the book!

BBS System: Online for 31 mins, 51 secs. Logged out at 27-Aug-88 20:24.

Steve and his Amiga-oriented BBS may be reached at 613-731-3419. The BBS now supports 2400 baud.

12
THE ONLY GOOD VIRUS IS A DEAD VIRUS

Will toys amuse when medicines cannot cure?
Reverend Edward Young (1683–1765)

"The basic rule is, where information can go, a virus can go with it," said Dr. Fred Cohen, a University of Cincinnati professor who has been doing research on the threat of computer viruses since 1983. He was quoted in an article in *The New York Times* that appeared on Sunday, January 31, 1988.

Dr. Cohen continues to point out that research performed by him in 1983 and 1984 has shown that most mainframe computers can be successfully subverted within an hour. Computer networks, even huge international ones with thousands of computers spread over continents, can be opened up to an illicit intruder within days.

The possibility of computer networks becoming a primary medium for subversion and warfare—the "softwar" depicted in a dozen classic science-fiction thrillers—"has become much more real," Dr. Cohen said.

It all becomes a matter of scale. Your neighbor is going to lose little sleep if a virus wipes out the files on the personal computer in your den. However, if his or her *bank's* data files are destroyed, not only your neighbor, but a lot of people are going to be demanding some answers about viruses.

Potential for Major Disasters

The practice of germ warfare, the deliberate release of deadly biological bacteria or viruses, is a practice so abhorrent it's firmly outlawed by international treaty. However, computer scientists, security experts, and computer users at all levels must now consider the possibility that something similar could be used to disable their systems.

Personal computers are the least of our worries.

Imagine the sudden shutdown of air traffic control, medical computers monitoring and running life support systems malfunctioning, financial networks penniless in the blink of an eye, widespread destruction of government and business records. We are now a computerized society at all levels and thus, particularly vulnerable to viruses.

"Suppose your virus attacked by deleting files in the system," Cohen said (this time in a report available in the public area of the Naval Weapons Support BBS and written by Lee Dembart). "If it started doing that right away, then as soon as your files got infected they would start to disappear and you'd say 'Hey, something's wrong here.' You'd probably be able to identify whoever did it."

To avoid early detection of the virus, a clever saboteur might add instructions to the virus program, causing it to check the date each time it ran. It would attack only if the date was identical to, or later than, some date months or years in the future. "Then," says Cohen, "one day, everything would stop. Even if they tried to replace the infected programs with programs that had been stored on backup tapes, the backup copies wouldn't work either—provided the copies were made after the system was infected."

The idea of virus-like programs has been around since at least 1975, when the science fiction writer John Brunner included one in his novel *The Shockwave Rider*. Brunner's "tapeworm" program ran loose through the computer network, gobbling up computer memory in order to duplicate itself. "It can't be killed," one character in the book exclaims in desperation. "It's indefinitely self-perpetuating as long as the network exists."

Two other experts were quoted in a report in *The New York Times.*

"A virus is deadly because it can jump—actually slide right through—the barriers everyone uses to control access to valuable information," said Kenneth Weiss, technical director at Security Dynamics Technologies Inc., a computer security division of the American Defense Preparedness Association. "The solution is to put a wall with a good solid gate around the jungle—most computers still have the equivalent of a sleepy guard at the door. But the larger problem is how to secure the system against people who have legitimate work inside."

"It's apparently going to be the game this year—to see who can come up with the best virus," said Dennis Steinaur, a senior security specialist at the National Bureau of Standards, which promotes computer security in nonmilitary Federal agencies and the private sector. "We've all very vulnerable."

Yet he said the bureau planned no immediate recommendations on the virus threat. "With limited resources," he said, "we like to put our priorities in areas where we can see solution."

Let's bo back to the public report by Lee Dembert from the Naval Weapons Support BBS.

Dembert writes that Marvin Schaefer, chief scientist at the Pentagon's computer security center, says the military has been concerned about penetration by virus-like programs for years. Defense planners have protected some top-secret computers by isolating them.

The secret computers of the military and such intelligence agencies as NSA and the National Reconnaissance Office are highly shielded electronically and connected to each other only when necessary by wires that run through pipes containing gas under pressure. Should anyone try to penetrate the pipes in order to tap into the wires, the drop in gas pressure would immediately cause an alarm. But, Schaefer admits, "in systems that don't have good access controls, there really is no way to contain a virus. It's quite possible for an attack to take over a machine."

Many in government and the computer industry very strongly believe that neither Cohen nor any other responsible expert should even open a public discussion of computer viruses. "It only takes a halfway decent programmer about half a day of thinking to figure out how to do it," Jerry Lobel of Honeywell says, as quoted in Dembart's article. "If you tell enough people about it, there's going to be one crazy enough out there who's going to try."

Cohen disagrees, insisting that it's more dangerous not to discuss and study computer viruses. "The point of these experiments," he says, "is that if I can figure out how to do it, somebody else can too. It's better to have somebody friendly do the experiment, tell you how bad it is, show you how it works and help you counteract it, than to have somebody vicious come along and do it." If you wait for the bad guys to create a virus first, Cohen says, then by the time you find out about it, it will be too late.

The Future of Viruses

In this book, we have been primarily concerned with viruses that attack personal computers. As stated earlier, one thing in our favor is that viruses are machine-specific. In other words, a Macintosh virus won't work on an IBM or compatible computer, and an Atari virus cannot inhabit a mainframe machine.

But, what if the personal computer program is merely a carrier for a virus that would infect *another* type of computer, such as a DEC VAX or an IBM System 370? Don't think this hasn't already occurred in the devious and twisted minds of virus-makers.

How does the virus get from the personal computer into the larger machine? Simplicity itself. We are now a world of networks. Millions of computers communicate with other computers. A mainframe virus concealed in a personal computer file could be easily transmitted to a mainframe.

Tomorrow you have no bank account. The morning after that, all the traffic lights in New York lock on red. That afternoon, an atomic power plant melts down.

Viruses are serious stuff.

There are no firm answers yet, no cut and dried guaranteed solutions. We are faced with electronic terrorism that could become horribly damaging to all of us, that could disrupt and endanger all of our lives. Everyone. Worldwide.

This book has been a start. Using the techniques and software described in these pages gives you a good measure of protection against viruses.

There are far more personal computers than mainframes, and all the media attention has been on the smaller computers. If we, as computer users, can all act responsibly to employ safe computing practices, we can halt the spread of computer viruses on IBM and compatibles, on Macs and Ataris, on Amigas and all the rest.

If those who concoct viruses are no longer getting publicity, maybe they'll quit. And maybe they won't make the effort to come up with viruses that can exist in a mainframe environment. Then all we have to worry about are disgruntled employees, and political terrorists, and foreign enemies.

Viruses are serious stuff.

We should be scared, and we should do something about it.

Good luck, and stomp a virus whenever you see it.

INDEX

COMPUTE! Books

Ask your retailer for these **COMPUTE! Books** or order directly from **COMPUTE!**.

Call toll free (in US) **1-800-346-6767** or write COMPUTE! Books, P.O. Box 2165, Radnor, PA 19089.

Quantity	Title	Price*	Total
_____	COMPUTE!'s Quick and Easy Guide to Borland's *Quattro* (C148X)	**$12.95**	_____
_____	COMPUTE!'s Quick and Easy Guide to Using MS-DOS (C1056)	**$12.95**	_____
_____	COMPUTE!'s Quick and Easy Guide to Learning *Lotus 1-2-3* (C1064)	**$12.95**	_____
_____	COMPUTE!'s Quick and Easy Guide to *AppleWorks* (C1099)	**$12.95**	_____
_____	COMPUTE!'s Quick and Easy Guide to *dBase III Plus* (C1072)	**$12.95**	_____
_____	COMPUTE!'s Quick and Easy Guide to *WordPerfect* (C0114)	**$12.95**	_____
_____	COMPUTE!'s Quick and Easy Guide to Desktop Publishing (C1129)	**$12.95**	_____
_____	COMPUTE!'s Quick and Easy Guide to Dow Jones News/Retrieval (C1137)	**$12.95**	_____
_____	COMPUTE!'s Quick & Easy Guide to *Microsoft Word* on the IBM (C1331)	**$12.95**	_____
_____	COMPUTE!'s Quick & Easy Guide to *Excel* on the Macintosh (C1315)	**$12.95**	_____
_____	COMPUTE!'s Quick & Easy Guide to *Microsoft Word* on the Macintosh (C1358)	**$12.95**	_____
_____	COMPUTE!'s Quick & Easy Guide to *R:Base System V* (C1322)	**$12.95**	_____
_____	COMPUTE!'s Quick & Easy Guide to OS/2 (C1374)	**$12.95**	_____
_____	COMPUTE!'s Quick & Easy Guide to *Lotus 1-2-3* Macros (C1412)	**$12.95**	_____
_____	COMPUTE!'s Quick & Easy Guide to PC *Excel* (C1404)	**$12.95**	_____
_____	COMPUTE!'s Quick & Easy Guide to *HyperCard* (C1455)	**$12.95**	_____

*Add $2.00 per book for shipping and handling.
Outside US add $5.00 air mail or $2.00 surface mail.

PA residents add 6% sales tax _____
Shipping & handling: $2.00/book _____
Total payment _____

All orders must be prepaid (check, charge, or money order).
All payments must be in US funds.
☐ Payment enclosed.
Charge ☐ Visa ☐ MasterCard ☐ American Express

Acct. No._____ Exp. Date_____
(Required)

Name_____

Address_____

City_____ State _____ Zip_____

*Allow 4–5 weeks for delivery.
Prices and availability subject to change.
Current catalog available upon request.

COMPUTE! Books

Ask your retailer for these **COMPUTE! Books** or order directly from **COMPUTE!**.

Call toll free (in US) **1-800-346-6767** or write COMPUTE! Books, P.O. Box 2165, Radnor, PA 19089.

Quantity	Title	Price*	Total
_____	The Official Book of *King's Quest* (C1552)	**$10.95**	_____
_____	40 Great *Flight Simulator* Adventures (C022X)	**$12.95**	_____
_____	40 More Great *Flight Simulator* Adventures (C0432)	**$12.95**	_____
	Flying on Instruments with *Flight Simulator*		
_____	perfect bound (C0912)	**$12.95**	_____
_____	wire bound (C103X)	**$12.95**	_____
	Jet Fighter School		
_____	perfect bound (C0920)	**$12.95**	_____
_____	COMPUTE!'s *Flight Simulator* Adventures for the Amiga, Atari ST, and Macintosh (C1005)	**$12.95**	_____
_____	Learning to Fly with *Flight Simulator* (C1153)	**$12.95**	_____
_____	The Electronic Battlefield (C117X)	**$12.95**	_____
_____	Sub Commander: Tactics and Strategy for WWII Submarine Simulations (C1277)	**$12.95**	_____
_____	Gunship Academy: Tactics and Maneuvers for Attack Helicopter Simulations (C1536)	**$12.95**	_____

*Add $2.00 per book for shipping and handling.
Outside US add $5.00 air mail or $2.00 surface mail.

PA residents add 6% sales tax _____
Shipping & handling: $2.00/book _____
Total payment _____

All orders must be prepaid (check, charge, or money order).
All payments must be in US funds.
☐ Payment enclosed.
Charge ☐ Visa ☐ MasterCard ☐ American Express

Acct. No._____ Exp. Date_____
(Required)

Name_____

Address_____

City_____ State _____ Zip_____

*Allow 4–5 weeks for delivery.
Prices and availability subject to change.
Current catalog available upon request.